Current
CONTROVERSIES

Child Abuse DISCARD

Other books in the Current Controversies series

Child Abuse

Lucinda Almond, Book Editor

GREENHAVEN PRESS

An imprint of Thomson Gale, a part of The Thomson Corporation

Detroit • New York • San Francisco • New Haven, Conn. • Waterville, Maine • London • Munich

THOMSON
™
GALE

Bonnie Szumski, *Publisher*
Helen Cothran, *Managing Editor*

© 2006 Thomson Gale, a part of The Thomson Corporation.

Thomson and Star logo are trademarks and Gale and Greenhaven Press are registered trademarks used herein under license.

For more information, contact:
Greenhaven Press
27500 Drake Rd.
Farmington Hills, MI 48331-3535
Or you can visit our Internet site at http://www.gale.com

Cover photograph reproduced by permission of Getty Images.

LIBRARY OF CONGRESS CATALOGING-IN-PUBLICATION DATA

Child Abuse / Lucinda Almond, book editor.
    p. cm. -- (Current controversies)
    Includes bibliographical references and index.
    ISBN 0-7377-2474-9 (hardcover lib. : alk. paper) -- ISBN 0-7377-2475-7 (pbk. : alk. paper)
    1. Child abuse. 2. Child abuse--United States. I. Almond, Lucinda. II. Series.
    HV6626.5.C4715 2007
    362.76--dc22
                                              2006016706

Printed in the United States of America
10 9 8 7 6 5 4 3 2 1

Contents

Chapter 1: Is Child Abuse a Serious Problem?

Yes: Child Abuse Is a Serious Problem

No: Child Abuse Is Not a Serious Problem

Chapter 2: What Factors Contribute to Child Abuse?

Chapter 4: Will Changes in the Criminal Justice System Help Prevent Child Abuse?

Foreword

By definition, controversies are "discussions of questions in which opposing opinions clash" (*Webster's Twentieth Century Dictionary Unabridged*). Few would deny that controversies are a pervasive part of the human condition and exist on virtually every level of human enterprise. Controversies transpire between individuals and among groups, within nations and between nations. Controversies supply the grist necessary for progress by providing challenges and challengers to the status quo. They also create atmospheres where strife and warfare can flourish. A world without controversies would be a peaceful world; but it also would be, by and large, static and prosaic.

The Series' Purpose

The purpose of the Current Controversies series is to explore many of the social, political, and economic controversies dominating the national and international scenes today. Titles selected for inclusion in the series are highly focused and specific. For example, from the larger category of criminal justice, Current Controversies deals with specific topics such as police brutality, gun control, white collar crime, and others. The debates in Current Controversies also are presented in a useful, timeless fashion. Articles and book excerpts included in each title are selected if they contribute valuable, long-range ideas to the overall debate. And wherever possible, current information is enhanced with historical documents and other relevant materials. Thus, while individual titles are current in focus, every effort is made to ensure that they will not become quickly outdated. Books in the Current Controversies series will remain important resources for librarians, teachers, and students for many years.

In addition to keeping the titles focused and specific, great care is taken in the editorial format of each book in the series. Book introductions and chapter prefaces are offered to provide background material for readers. Chapters are organized around several key questions that are answered with diverse opinions representing all points on the political spectrum. Materials in each chapter include opinions in which authors clearly disagree as well as alternative opinions in which authors may agree on a broader issue but disagree on the possible solutions. In this way, the content of each volume in Current Controversies mirrors the mosaic of opinions encountered in society. Readers will quickly realize that there are many viable answers to these complex issues. By questioning each author's conclusions, students and casual readers can begin to develop the critical thinking skills so important to evaluating opinionated material.

Current Controversies is also ideal for controlled research. Each anthology in the series is composed of primary sources taken from a wide gamut of informational categories including periodicals, newspapers, books, United States and foreign government documents, and the publications of private and public organizations. Readers will find factual support for reports, debates, and research papers covering all areas of important issues. In addition, an annotated table of contents, an index, a book and periodical bibliography, and a list of organizations to contact are included in each book to expedite further research.

Perhaps more than ever before in history, people are confronted with diverse and contradictory information. During the Persian Gulf War, for example, the public was not only treated to minute-to-minute coverage of the war, it was also inundated with critiques of the coverage and countless analyses of the factors motivating U.S. involvement. Being able to sort through the plethora of opinions accompanying today's major issues, and to draw one's own conclusions, can be a complicated and frustrating struggle. It is the editors' hope that Current Controversies will help readers with this struggle.

Introduction

"Justice, dignity, equality—these are words which are often used loosely, with little appreciation of their meaning. I think that their meaning can be distilled into one goal: that every child in this country live as we would want our own children to live."

—*Robert F. Kennedy,*
New York, 1965

Police found eighteen-month-old Brodie Ansley on the living room floor. She was covered with bruises, had swollen eyes, and had been dead for about twelve hours. The baby's mother, twenty-one-year-old Amrin Ansley, confessed that she heard her boyfriend, eighteen-year-old Jeremiah Sergio Ayala, abusing her child in another room, but she did not try to stop him, nor did she check on her child. Ayala later admitted to striking the baby, shaking her, throwing her, and picking her up by her neck. He was angry with her for crying but admitted that the abuse probably would not have occurred if he had not been drunk. Brodie was the fifth child to die as a result of child abuse during the first forty-eight days of 2006 in Clark County, Nevada.

The death of a child so young is shocking, but child fatalities are only one consequence of such abuse. Another serious impact is injury. According to the National Clearinghouse on Child Abuse and Neglect Information, child abuse is defined as the "physical injury (ranging from minor bruises to severe fractures or death) as a result of punching, beating, kicking, biting, shaking, throwing, stabbing, choking, hitting (with a hand, stick, strap, or other object), burning, or otherwise harming a child. Such injury is considered abuse regardless of whether the caretaker intended to hurt the child." Many of these injuries leave lifetime scars that can never be repaired. For instance, long-term consequences of shaken baby syndrome include blindness, mental retardation, paralysis, or cerebral palsy. Physical abuse can also cause attention deficit/ hyperactivity disorder, anxiety, and memory impairment.

Child abuse of any type also creates long-term emotional trauma for the child. The child learns not to trust others, which can result in fear and depression. Researchers have identified links between abuse and mental/emotional health problems. Child abuse victims have been found to be 25 percent more likely to experience delinquency, teen pregnancy, and drug use. Some studies show that as many as 80 percent of abused children have at least one psychiatric disorder by the age of twenty-one. Some of these disorders include low self-esteem, eating disorders, and suicide attempts. Other studies link multiple personality disorders to early child sexual abuse. Additionally, many researchers support the hypothesis that sexual abuse greatly disrupts the child's developing sexuality and places the victim at risk for adult sexual problems. In regard to their personal relationships as adults, child abuse victims exhibit a general instability in their intimate relationships and are at greater risk for divorce or separation from a spouse. Victims often express an overall lower level of satisfaction in their close relationships. The breach of trust that these victims experienced as children often interferes with their abilities to form secure attachments to others.

Cognitive development, too, is negatively impacted by child abuse. Child abuse experiences may cause delays or deficits in a child's ability to achieve age-appropriate behavioral, cognitive, and emotional regulation. Victims of abuse consistently perform at a lower level in school, as evidenced by grade point averages, standardized test scores, language skills, verbal ability, and frequent retention in the same grade. Many studies show that almost half of abused/neglected kindergartners are referred to special education programs or are required to repeat the grade. Confusion, lower IQ, learning disabilities, development delays, high absenteeism rates, and poor social skills have all been linked to child abuse and/or neglect. The victims tend to view themselves as unworthy and incompetent, which often leads to a lack of motivation to succeed in school. Teachers report that victims are more likely to be disorganized, distracted, impulsive, angry, and noncompliant in terms of behavior. All of these factors contribute to the child's poor performance in school, which later leads to high dropout rates. Up to 75 percent of high school dropouts come from abusive homes.

The effects of abuse on children are also felt by the community as a whole. Victims of abuse have a higher rate of criminal behavior than non-abused children. According to the Prevent Child Abuse organization, 80 percent of violent juvenile and adult prisoners were raised in violent homes. Additionally, survivors of abuse are six times more likely to become abusive parents. Numerous studies over the years have demonstrated that boys who grow up in violent homes are likely to become batterers. As teens, they beat their girlfriends. Karen Maxwell, Sacramento, California's supervising prosecutor at Juvenile Hall, believes that children who come from abusive homes have no respect for themselves, their mothers, or anyone else. "We see kids who come through who don't seem to have a soul," she said. "They have love for no one." James Gilligan, author of *Violence: Our Deadly Epidemic and Its Causes*, argues that prevention, not punishment, is the solution to violent crimes. Gilligan has studied violent prisoners for more than twenty years and concludes that the most brutal inmates have suffered extraordinary abuse during childhood. Such abuse results in the feeling that the essence of who they are has been destroyed. Virtually all inmates said that they are emotionally dead or numb. This lack of guilt triggers their criminal behavior, often including murder.

In addition to the violence that society experiences due to child abuse, the economic costs of such abuse is staggering. The state of Michigan undertook a study that compared the costs of abuse prevention services with the costs for the consequences of child abuse. The study showed a 19 to 1 cost advantage to prevention. The study took into account the costs for premature babies, infant mortality, special education, protective services, foster care, juvenile and adult criminality, and psychological services. The study also included the costs of medical care for injuries, substance abuse treatment for survivors, police, prosecution, incarceration, legal expenses, and case workers. Other hidden costs were not examined, such as the costs for lost productivity in the workforce.

These far-reaching consequences demonstrate the urgent need for child abuse prevention programs. The authors of *Current Controversies: Child Abuse* debate the causes of child abuse and offer possible ways to address it. Those working to prevent child abuse—even though they often disagree about the most effective methods—have one common goal: to ensure that every child has a chance at a good life.

Is Child Abuse a Serious Problem?

Chapter Preface

In March 2002 Mary took her eleven-year-old daughter to a pediatrician's office to seek a diagnosis for the girl's persistent stomach cramps. After an examination the doctor ordered a pregnancy test, which came back positive. During separate visits the doctor questioned both the girl and Mary about the child's sexual activity and inquired about any boyfriends the girl might have had. Both the girl and her mother denied any sexual history, and the girl denied that anyone had ever touched her inappropriately. During this time an anonymous caller contacted the police to report that the man who impregnated the girl was a man in his seventies whom the girl had been paired with through an Adopt-a-Grandparent program. The man was later arrested and had several charges filed against him, including fourth-degree sexual assault. Prosecutors also filed charges against the doctor for failing to report the abuse.

The role of doctors in reporting child abuse lies at the center of debates about how prevalent such abuse is. Those who believe that child abuse is more widespread than statistics indicate argue that the doctors underreport abuse, thereby skewing the statistics. On the other side of the controversy are those who say that doctors often report child abuse when no abuse has in fact occurred.

Everyone agrees that child abuse is a horrific crime, but controversy arises when it comes to how prevalent the problem really is. The National Child Abuse and Neglect Data System reported an estimated fourteen hundred child fatalities in 2002 due to abuse or neglect. Many researchers believe that these numbers are too low. Deaths classified as accidents or sudden infant death syndrome (SIDS) may actually be the result of abuse or neglect, they claim, and they argue that comprehensive investigations and consistent consensus of what constitutes abuse/neglect are needed in order to obtain accurate statistics. Studies in two states have estimated that as many as 60 percent of abuse/neglect deaths are not reported.

In their article "Barriers to Physician Identification and Reporting of Child Abuse," Emalee G. Flaherty and Robert Sege speculate that many doctors may not be familiar with abuse symptoms. Race and socioeconomic status may also play a role in doctors' decisions to report suspected abuse. The authors noted one study in which black children were up to seven times more likely to be reported as abuse victims than were white children. However, white children were more likely to be reported to authorities if they came from a lower socioeconomic class. Additionally, doctors who were tolerant of physical punishment were less likely to suspect that an injury was caused by abuse. Vague state laws, lack of access to child abuse experts, lack of training, and fear of malpractice suits are further reasons why many doctors do not report abuse.

On the other side of the debate, the media has reported many cases over the years in which society appears to be on a witch hunt for abusers, often resulting in the conviction of innocent people. Those who claim that child abuse is overreported argue that laws often require doctors to report abuse, and physicians are often afraid not to, even when they are not absolutely sure abuse has occurred. Many commentators also claim that making a diagnosis of child abuse has become a fad among mental health care professionals. These commentators say that overzealous psychologists convince their patients that abuse has occurred, even when such incidents cannot be substantiated. When these cases are publicized, other psychologists read about such cases and begin to wonder if the problems experienced by their own patients might be caused by abuse. Many decide in the affirmative even though they have no substantive proof.

No one will contest the assertion that child abuse is horrifying, but experts on both sides of the issue argue intently over its extent. The authors in the following chapter present some of the arguments from both sides of the controversy.

Child Abuse in the United States Is a Serious Problem

National Clearinghouse on Child Abuse and Neglect Information

The National Clearinghouse on Child Abuse and Neglect Information was established in 1974 by the Child Abuse Prevention and Treatment Act to collect, organize, and disseminate information on all aspects of child maltreatment.

Despite the efforts of the child protection system, child maltreatment fatalities remain a serious problem. Although the untimely deaths of children due to illness and accidents have been closely monitored, deaths that result from physical assault or severe neglect can be more difficult to track. Intervention strategies targeted at resolving this problem face complex challenges.

The National Child Abuse and Neglect Data System (NCANDS) reported an estimated 1,400 child fatalities in 2002. This translates to a rate of 1.98 children per 100,000 children in the general population. NCANDS defines "child fatality" as the death of a child caused by an injury resulting from abuse or neglect, or where abuse or neglect were contributing factors.

Many researchers and practitioners believe child fatalities due to abuse and neglect are underreported. States' definitions of key terms such as "child homicide," "abuse," and "neglect" vary (therefore, so do the numbers and types of child fatalities they report). In addition, some deaths officially labeled as accidents, child homicides, and/or Sudden Infant Death Syndrome (SIDS) might be attributed to child abuse or neglect if

National Clearinghouse on Child Abuse and Neglect Information, "Child Abuse and Neglect Fatalities, Statistics and Interventions," http://nccanch.acf.hhs.gov, April 2004. Reproduced by permission.

more comprehensive investigations were conducted or if there were more consensus in the coding of abuse on death certificates.

The Number of Deaths Is Underreported

Studies in Colorado and North Carolina have estimated as many as 50 to 60 percent of deaths resulting from abuse or neglect are not recorded. These studies indicate that neglect is the most underrecorded form of fatal maltreatment.

In 2002, one or both parents were involved in 79 percent of child abuse or neglect fatalities.

The rate of child abuse and neglect fatalities reported by NCANDS has increased slightly over the last several years from 1.84 per 100,000 children in 2000 to 1.96 in 2001 and 1.98 in 2002. However, experts do not agree whether this represents an actual increase in child abuse and neglect fatalities, or whether it may be attributed to improvements in reporting procedures. For example, statistics on approximately 20 percent of fatalities were from health departments and fatality review boards for 2002, compared to 11.4 percent for 2001, an indication of greater coordination of data collection among agencies.

A number of issues affecting the accuracy and consistency of child fatality data from year to year have been identified, including:

- Variation among reporting requirements and definitions of child abuse and neglect.

- Variation in State child fatality review processes.

- The amount of time (as long as a year, in some cases) it may take a fatality review team to declare abuse or neglect as the cause of death.

- Miscoding of death certificates.

Babies Are at Higher Risk

Research indicates very young children (ages 3 and younger) are the most frequent victims of child fatalities. NCANDS data for 2002 demonstrated children younger than 1 year accounted for 41 percent of fatalities, while children younger than 4 years accounted for 76 percent of fatalities. This population of children is the most vulnerable for many reasons, including their dependency, small size, and inability to defend themselves.

In 2002, more than one-third (38 percent) of child maltreatment fatalities were associated with neglect alone. Physical abuse alone was cited in more than one-quarter (30 percent) of reported fatalities. Another 29 percent of fatalities were the result of multiple maltreatment types.

Fatal child abuse may involve repeated abuse over a period of time (e.g., battered child syndrome), or it may involve a single, impulsive incident (e.g., drowning, suffocating, or shaking a baby). In cases of fatal neglect, the child's death results not from anything the caregiver does, but from a caregiver's *failure to act*. The neglect may be chronic (e.g., extended malnourishment) or acute (e.g., an infant who drowns because she is left unsupervised in the bathtub).

Who Are the Abusers?

No matter how the fatal abuse occurs, one fact of great concern is that the perpetrators are, by definition, individuals responsible for the care and supervision of their victims. In 2002, one or both parents were involved in 79 percent of child abuse or neglect fatalities. Of the other 21 percent of fatalities, 16 percent were the result of maltreatment by nonparent caretakers, and 5 percent were unknown or missing. These percentages are consistent with findings from previous years.

There is no single profile of a perpetrator of fatal child abuse, although certain characteristics reappear in many studies. Frequently the perpetrator is a young adult in his or her mid-20s without a high school diploma, living at or below the poverty level, depressed, and who may have difficulty coping with stressful situations. In many instances, the perpetrator has experienced violence first-hand. Most fatalities from *physical abuse* are caused by fathers and other male caretakers. Mothers are most often held responsible for deaths resulting from *child neglect*. However, in some cases this may be because women are most often responsible (or assumed to be responsible) for children's care.

When addressing the issue of child maltreatment, and especially child fatalities, prevention is a recurring theme.

The response to the problem of child abuse and neglect fatalities is often hampered by inconsistencies, including:

- Inaccurate reporting of the number of children who die each year as a result of abuse and neglect.

- Lack of national standards for child autopsies or death investigations.

- The different roles child protective services (CPS) agencies in different jurisdictions play in the investigation process.

- The use in some States of medical examiners or elected coroners who do not have specific child abuse and neglect training.

Review Teams Enhance Investigations

To address some of these inconsistencies, multidisciplinary/ multiagency child fatality review teams have emerged to provide a coordinated approach to the investigation of child deaths. These teams, which now exist at a State, local, or State/ local level in every State and the District of Columbia, are comprised of prosecutors, coroners or medical examiners, law enforcement personnel, CPS workers, public health care providers, and others. Child fatality review teams offer many benefits, including improved interagency communication, identification of gaps in community child protection systems, and the development of data information systems that can guide agency policy and practice.

The teams review cases of child deaths and facilitate appropriate follow-up. Follow-up may include ensuring that services are provided for surviving family members, providing information to assist in the prosecution of perpetrators, and developing recommendations to improve child protection and community support systems.

When addressing the issue of child maltreatment, and especially child fatalities, prevention is a recurring theme. Well-designed, properly organized child fatality review teams appear to offer hope for defining the underlying nature and scope of fatalities due to child abuse and neglect. The child fatality review process helps identify risk factors that may assist prevention professionals, such as those engaged in home visiting and parenting education, to prevent future deaths.

Awareness Is Critical

In 2003, the Office on Child Abuse and Neglect, within the Children's Bureau, Administration for Children and Families, U.S. Department of Health and Human Services, launched a Child Abuse Prevention Initiative to raise awareness of the issue in a much more visible and comprehensive way than ever before. The Prevention Initiative is an opportunity to work together in communities across the country to keep children safe, provide the support families need to stay together, and raise children and youth to be happy, secure, and stable adults. . . .

While the exact number of children affected is uncertain, child fatalities due to abuse and neglect remain a serious problem in the United States. Fatalities disproportionately affect young children and are most often caused by one or both of the child's parents. Child fatality review teams appear to be among the most promising current approaches to responding to and preventing child abuse and neglect fatalities.

Trafficking in Children Is a Serious Problem

Carla Power, Liat Radcliffe, and Karen MacGregor

Carla Power, Liat Radcliffe, and Karen MacGregor are staff writers for Newsweek International.

O ver pasta in a Bloomsbury pizzeria, "Maria" could pass for any urban 21-year-old Londoner. She's not. The Macedonia-born Maria was orphaned at 9, then sent to stay with a family whose 19-year-old son, "Nuri," began sleeping with her. He bought her a new dress and a doll, and then trafficked her through southern Europe to what was billed simply as "a better life" in Italy. On arrival, Nuri told Maria they needed money. "That's all right," she responded. "I can make lace." But within a day of her arrival Maria, then 10, was on the streets of Milan. For the next couple of years she was sold as a virgin. "I used to put a chicken liver inside me," she says. "Old prostitute's trick." At 15 she accompanied Nuri and eight other pimps and their child prostitutes and drove to England. She spent the next few years working the length of the British Isles, servicing clients 18 hours a day, seven days a week. "Whatever they wanted they got," she says.

Forced Slavery

Maria's story of indentured servitude is increasingly common. Over the last decade, thousands of kids from all over the world have been smuggled into Europe to do dirty work. In September [2003] police arrested a couple in the southern Italian region of Calabria for allegedly buying an Albanian boy from a Durresrun trafficking gang, one of a clutch of gangs involved in supplying Italians with Albanian kids for illegal adoptions. Eastern Europe's girls are trafficked for the sex industry, while its boys work either as male prostitutes or in petty crime. Chinese children are trafficked to work in European sweatshops or on the streets. West African kids are sneaked into Europe to work as domestic servants, or for use in benefit-fraud schemes or ritual sacrifices for tribal African religions. The 2001 discovery of a Nigerian boy's torso in the Thames led British police to arrest 21 suspected traffickers. . . .

Globalization, post-Soviet poverty and the European Union's [EU's] newly porous borders have made child trafficking the world's fastest-growing branch of organized crime. Reliable statistics are scant, but the United Nations puts the worldwide number of children trafficked at 1.2 million a year. A 2001 EU study estimated that 120,000 women and children are clandestinely brought into Western Europe annually.

Whether Albanian or Nigerian or Chinese, the traffickers prey on poverty and ignorance.

Police organizations take the problem seriously, but investigations are often handicapped by Europe's fragmented legal system. Laws on trafficking and migration vary enormously among the EU's 15 member countries. And with 10 new members set to join the Union—many of them, like Hungary, source countries for trafficked women and children—there are sure to be new complications. [We] could see a huge rise in Eastern European young people heading to Western Europe, where they'll be vulnerable to exploitation, fears Lars Loof of the Children's Unit at the Council for Baltic States. "In a larger Europe, it's naturally even easier for under-18s to go across borders without authorities' knowing," he says.

Some Laws Punish the Victims

Legal loopholes can leave victims unprotected and traffickers unpunished. Until recently the Greeks arrested child-trafficking victims. [In 2003] the U.S. State Department threatened Greece with sanctions if it didn't improve its counter-trafficking policies. The country has since promised a program of victim assistance. Italy has led Europe with progressive legislation on humanitarian visas to ensure that victims aren't repatriated and retrafficked and [it] passed a tough law equating trafficking with slavery.

Worried that trafficking will only grow in the years ahead, Europe knows a more coordinated approach is needed. Last year's [2002's] Brussels Declaration was the EU's first attempt to develop a comprehensive policy on trafficking that includes prevention, punishment and rehabilitation of the victims. [In 2003] EU Justice and Home Affairs ministers agreed to grant limited-term visas to trafficked people who cooperate with police. Source countries, including Croatia and Hungary, have started countertrafficking campaigns. But success is a relative term. "If a government can say, 'We've raided 150 brothels and pulled out 300 women without passports,' they can show a concrete, measurable response to the problem," notes Lisa Kurbiel, UNICEF's [the United Nations children's program's] project officer for child trafficking. "But that doesn't address the root causes."

Poor Children Targeted

Whether Albanian or Nigerian or Chinese, the traffickers prey on poverty and ignorance. "The trade has really grown recently, mainly because of the downward trend of economic development [in West Africa]," says UNICEF's Dakar-based spokesperson Margherita Amodeo. "Families that don't have anything are the most vulnerable." But other regional issues—a lack of education, the low status of girls, weak legal systems—also contribute to the problem. *Vidomegon*, a common West African practice in which families send children to live with wealthier relatives or friends to get a better education, is one way traffickers find and acquire kids.

[In 2002] Maria walked out on her pimp with £20 in her pocket. She's now got three years of humanitarian protection and a place at Cambridge University. Few stories finish as happily as hers. Most child victims end up dead, enslaved or on drugs. Migrant advocates say Britain's tough stance against immigration and asylum seekers will only fuel the trafficking trade. "Every time they clamp down, they put women and children at risk," says Diana Mills of the London-based NGO [nongovernmental organization] Asylum Aid. "As soon as people go underground, they fall into the hands of the traffickers. The government is playing right into their hands." Without laws that protect trafficking victims instead of punishing them, a newly enlarged Europe won't just bring freedom. For thousands of children like Maria, it could mean slavery.

Internet Child Pornography Is a Growing Problem

Ron Scherer

Ron Scherer is a staff writer for the Christian Science Monitor.

Despite highly publicized arrests, law-enforcement officials say that the sexual exploitation of children on the Internet is growing dramatically.

[Between 2001 and 2004,] the number of reports of child pornography sites to the National Center for Missing & Exploited Children (NCMEC) [grew] by almost 400 percent. Law-enforcement officials are particularly disturbed by the increased number of commercial sites that offer photos of exploited children in return for a credit-card number. Those fighting child porn say it has become a global multibillion-dollar industry.

"We are encountering staggering proportions of violators or offenders we would have never imagined years ago," says Ray Smith, who oversees child exploitation investigations by the United States Postal Inspection Service. "It is an exploding problem worldwide, and particularly in the US," adds Ernie Allen, president of NCMEC.

Efforts to stem the upsurge are taking place on multiple fronts. At [a] summit in Scotland [in July 2005], officials said that Interpol, an international police organization, is putting together a global database of offenders and victims. [In August 2005] 3,000 law-enforcement officials from around the [United States met] in Dallas to discuss ways to attack Internet crimes against children.

On the state level, New Jersey and Florida are among those enacting requirements for [convicted] sexual predators to wear GPS [global positioning satellite] devices that keep track of their whereabouts.

Stop the Money Flow

One of the biggest pushes against the purveyors is aimed at shutting down the use of credit cards. NCMEC is currently talking to MasterCard about making it even harder to subscribe to the commercial sites.

"We're trying to mobilize the financial industry to choke off the money," says Mr. Allen.

At MasterCard, spokeswoman Sharon Gamsin says her organization is "appalled people are using our systems for illegal transactions involving child pornography, and finding a way to stop this is a priority."

[In 2003] Visa International began a program to try to identify child porn sites allowing transactions with its credit cards. It hired a firm that used retired federal agents to go through the Internet searching for sites, and it says it's still searching the Web for illicit sites today.

Officials generally give the credit-card companies good marks for their efforts. "The financial industry is made up of real people with children, and they want this thing ended for society, too," says Mr. Smith, who has been fighting the illegal merchandise since 1982.

To try to help credit-card companies and law-enforcement officials identify websites, NCMEC has hired a consultant to search online for illicit sites. "We provide the information first to law enforcement and then do reviews to see if they follow up," he says. "Otherwise, we send a cease-and-desist order to the method-of-payment services [such as a credit-card company] and try to engage banks and regulators." Allen notes that he recently met with Asian bankers to seek cooperation.

Shutting off the money flow could help, agree officials. Jim Plitt, director of the US Immigration and Customs Enforcement (ICE) Cyber Crime Center, believes that the growth of the child porn industry is part of what he terms the "illegal business cycle"—where groups watching the huge profits decide to join in.

"The emphasis is on the money. That's where you focus," says Mr. Plitt, who adds, "more cases are coming."

When law-enforcement officials have cracked the organizations, they often find that the organizations have many illegal websites that are collecting money. That was the case with Regpay, a company in Minsk, Belarus, which provided credit-card billing services for 50 child porn websites worldwide.

International Pedophile Club

Indeed, the groups are often international in scope. The Regpay investigation resulted in the initial arrests of 35 people in the United States, France, and Spain. "The actual businesses themselves are not necessarily large, but they have a large membership pool," says Plitt.

When Regpay was broken up [in 2003], it had 270,000 subscribers—4,000 in New Jersey alone. Recently, in fact, 11 more individual subscribers were arrested in New Jersey, and more arrests are on the way, say officials.

Because the membership pool was so large, law-enforcement officials have broken the prosecutions down into two phases. The first phase was to dismantle the financial apparatus, including businesses in Florida and California that processed US credit-card transactions. The second phase, which is ongoing, is to arrest individuals who subscribed to the sites.

"The [arrests] are prioritized, so we are targeting individuals with access to children, people of trust in the community, and the most egregious subscribers who had lots of transactions," says Jamie Zuieback, a spokeswoman for ICE. "What you'll see in the cases made are schoolteachers, pediatricians, a campus minister, a Boy Scout leader, and other individuals in those types of positions."

ICE is now arresting individuals who subscribed to the sites multiple times.

Although the arrests themselves get the word out to the pedophile community, some law-enforcement officials are optimistic that technology may ultimately help them stem the tide. "I think there will come a time in the not-too-distant future where, working with the [Internet service provider] community and the financial community, they will be able to package information and put it into computers that will not allow people to subscribe to these sites," says Smith.

The Catholic Church Routinely Ignores Child Sexual Abuse by Clergy

Edd Doerr

Edd Doerr, president of Americans for Religious Liberty, is the author of more than 3,000 published books, articles, columns, translations, letters, short stories, and poems.

On July 23, 2003, Massachusetts Attorney General Thomas F. Reilly released a groundbreaking and finely detailed report entitled "The Sexual Abuse of Children in the Roman Catholic Archdiocese of Boston." (The eighty-four page report is available in its entirety on the attorney general's website at www.ago.state.ma.us/archdiocese.pdf.)

In January 2002, Catholic priest John Geoghan was convicted of molesting a boy and sentenced to ten years in prison. More than 130 people had accused him of sexual abuse over a period of many years; other criminal charges, as well as several civil lawsuits, were pending against him. Geoghan's case is important because it led to the exposure of massive scandals regarding clerical sex abuse of minors.

Clerical sexual abuse of minors in Massachusetts is of public concern because it is a serious crime, as is the coverup of such abuse by ecclesiastical authorities. And such sexual abuse isn't confined to Massachusetts or the United States, but it is a long-festering worldwide problem of staggering magnitude.

A Massive Cover-Up

Sexual abuse of minors isn't confined to Catholic priests or even to clergy generally. Parents, relatives, teachers, scout lead-

Edd Doerr, "A Culture of Clergy Sexual Abuse," *The Humanist*, vol. 63, November–December 2003, p. 41. Copyright 2003 American Humanist Association. Reproduced by permission.

ers, various authority figures, and strangers are also guilty of these crimes. But nowhere has the abuse of minors been so protected or systematically covered up as in the nation's and the world's largest top-down-run religious organization. And rank-and-file Catholics are just as concerned about this problem as anyone else.

In his introduction to the report, Reilly states:

> Based on my conclusions and in order to ensure that children will be safe in the future, this report is essential; it is essential to create an official public record of what occurred. This mistreatment of children was so massive and so prolonged that it borders on the unbelievable. This report will confirm to all who may read it now and in the future, that this tragedy was real.

Reilly states that [Boston] archdiocese records show "that at least 789 victims (or third parties acting on the behalf of victims) have complained directly to the Archdiocese," that the "number of alleged victims who have disclosed their abuse likely exceeds one thousand. And the number increases even further when considering that an unknown number of victims likely have not, and may never disclose their abuses to others."

Reilly's report adds:

> For more than fifty years there has been an institutional acceptance within the Archdiocese of clergy sexual abuse of children. Clergy sexual abuse of children has also been shown to be a nationwide problem with some reports indicating that more than 300 priests were removed from ministry in 2002 alone as a result of allegations of sexual abuse of children, and as many as 1,200 Roman Catholic priests in the United States have been accused of sexually abusing more than 4,000 children. The staggering magnitude of the problem would have alerted any reasonable, responsible manager that immediate and decisive measures must be taken.

Molesters Are Protected

The report adds that the archdiocese's "investigation and discipline process ... protects priests at the expense of victims and, in the final analysis, is incapable of leading to timely and appropriate responses to sex abuse allegations."

Reilly's report concludes:

> The Archdiocese's responses to reports of sexual abuse of children, including maintaining secrecy of reports, placed children at risk. Top Archdiocese officials ... decided that they should conceal—from the parishes, the laity, law enforcement and the public—their knowledge of individual complaints of abuse and the long history of such complaints within the Archdiocese. ... The Archdiocese believed that Canon Law—the church's internal policies and procedures—prohibited it from reporting abuse to civil authorities in most instances ... and the resulting publicity would harm the reputation of the Church. ... In the very few cases where allegations of sexual abuse of children were communicated to law enforcement, senior Archdiocese managers remained committed to their primary objectives—safeguarding the well-being of priests and the institution over the welfare of children and preventing scandal—and often failed to advise law enforcement authorities of all relevant information they possessed, including the full extent of the alleged abuser's history of abusing children.

An appendix to Reilly's report shows that between 1994 and 2000 the Boston archdiocese paid out $17,870,482 to settle legal claims from 402 victims, plus $1,157,219 for treatment costs to victims and $702,770 for treatment of priest abusers. Extrapolating from this data, it seems reasonable to agree with published estimates that since 1990 Catholic dioceses in the United States have paid out more than $1 billion to abuse victims—and that may only be the beginning.

In late August 2003 the Catholic Diocese of Covington, Kentucky, one of the church's smaller judicatories, released a report showing that since 1989 it had paid nearly $780,000 to abuse victims, $722,000 for counseling, and $218,000 in legal fees. The diocese also announced that it would begin talking with twenty-two people who have filed a $50 million suit charging clergy sex abuse. The Covington diocese also disclosed that 8 percent (30 of 372) of diocesan priests had sexually abused one or more minors over the past 50 years. . . .

The number of victims worldwide will never be known but certainly goes well into the many tens of thousands.

Thousands Abused

Reilly's report confirms and is confirmed by the extraordinary and important book *Pederasty in the Catholic Church: Sexual Crimes of the Clergy Against Minors, a Drama Silenced and Covered Up by the Bishops* . . . by Spanish psychologist Pepe Rodriguez. Rodriguez covers pretty much the same ground as Reilly, but in greater depth and scope, replete with case histories, covering not only the United States but also Spain, Latin America, and elsewhere.

Rodriguez' book, up to date as of September 2002, makes clear that the problem of sexual abuse of minors by religious authority figures is aggravated by two factors: the understandable reluctance of victims to report abuse and the longstanding but largely unwritten policy of church officials, from the pope on down, to coddle abusers and go to great lengths to cover up abuse. Both Rodriguez . . . and Reilly . . . detail the church policy of transferring abusers from one parish to another, one diocese to another, and even one country to another.

Rodriguez notes that various estimates of the number of priests, and even bishops, who abuse minors range from 3 percent to 6 percent, though the figure for Spain may be even higher, with the Covington, Kentucky, diocese weighing in at 8 percent. The number of victims worldwide will never be known but certainly goes well into the many tens of thousands.

Most Priests Are Sexually Active

Rodriguez' 2002 book builds on his 1995 book, *The Sex Life of the Clergy*. In this remarkably thorough earlier book, the Spanish pychologist covers even broader ground. His studies in traditionally Catholic Spain show that 60 percent of priests are sexually active in violation of their celibacy vows. Of these, his study found, 53 percent had relations with adult females, 21 percent with adult males, 14 percent with minor males, and 12 percent with minor females. He notes that a large number of Spanish priests left the priesthood to marry and that others formed long-term relationships ignored by both the laity and the church hierarchy. . . .

Rodriguez recommends that instances of sexual abuse be reported to police or civil authorities, as complaining to church authorities is likely to lead nowhere, though hopefully the expanding scandal . . . might possibly improve the situation.

False Allegations of Child Sexual Abuse Are Common

Dean Tong

Dean Tong is a forensic consultant and author.

Not only are children victims of real abuse, but also of the parental alienation or SAID [sexual allegations in divorce] syndromes, where the abuse-excuse is used as a tactic or bargaining chip by one parent seeking divorce and/or child custody. Studies indicate that malicious false child abuse allegations made in bad faith occur [approximately] 2%–5% of the time. Many of the same, according to Ira Turkat, Ph.D., occur globally and as a result of Divorce-Related "Malicious Moms" Syndrome.

Recent research indicates that most unfounded claims of sexual child abuse are fostered by "delusional" accusers. [Julia A.] Hickman & [Cecil R.] Reynolds, in their paper entitled "Effects of False Allegations of Sexual Abuse on Children and Families," believe delusional accusers, usually mothers, may suffer from a mental health condition such as Borderline Personality Disorder (BPD), and they will shop for an expert to confirm their child has been abused, and will not take NO for an answer! Some accusers use the psychological phenomena of projection and transference to convince the "abused" child . . . Daddy touched you in bad places!. . .

Pathological Lying

Dr. Charles Ford, a psychiatrist and author of the book *Lies, Lies, Lies: The Psychology of Deceit* (American Psychiatric Press, 1999) refers to a phenomenon known as "Pseudologia Fantastica," or pathological lying. . . . These fantastic liars, who are

Dean Tong. http://www.abuse-excuse.com/ae_home.html. 2005. Reproduced by permission.

not the same as delusional psychotics, according to Dr. Ford, about 1/3 of the time will suffer some form of brain dysfunction. He says that "such liars are often smooth-talking narcissists, so self-centered they often think they can construct a reality. In many instances, the lying gets worse as the liar gets more power." . . .

Recent studies conducted by [Stephen J.] Ceci, [Maggie] Bruck, [C.M.] McBrien, and [Dale] Dagenbach have shed light on two highly probable reasons for the vast number of unfounded and erroneous child abuse reports; [namely,] confirmatory bias (whereby social services and the authorities have a pre-conceived notion the abuse already occurred when they undertake an investigation) and source misattributions (whereby the children and "professionals" misattribute the source or origin of the so-called abuse). . . .

In addition, Dr. Ceci, et al. have developed a new test to determine the extent, or lack thereof, of suggestibility and memory recall relative to individual differences in children [of] at least the age of four and one-half. Called the Video Suggestibility Scale for Children, it could be an important tool for child protection workers, psychologists, and attorneys, . . . especially in cases where kids change their stories.

Two-Thirds of Cases Are Unconfirmed

In 2002, as reported by the National Center on Child Abuse and Neglect, of the 2.6 million reports of alleged child abuse and neglect in America, 66%, or 2/3 were unconfirmed or unsubstantiated. . . .

According to a . . . study by the Department of Justice and conducted by Dr. David Finkelhor from the National Crimes Against Children Laboratory in Durham, New Hampshire, the incidence of sexual child abuse declined 40% between 1992 and 2000. . . .

Non-Abused Children Become Victims

Lacking the necessary education and training skills to conduct objective and competent child protective "investigations," intake workers at social service agencies remove non-abused children from their homes frequently: and in doing so, leave truly abused children in jeopardy. Combine this equation with a mental health industry that is rendering unnecessary clinical therapies for alleged repressed memories, and you have a prescription for disaster.

We will not win the war against child abuse until we first win the battle against false accusations.

To exacerbate matters, our triers-of-facts, our courts, [are] rubber stamping error-rich recommendations from guardians-ad-litem, social services, child protection teams, and therapists . . . forcing non-abused children into foster care homes while allowing kids in harm's way to die (at the hands of the state).

[Numerous high-profile, widely publicized] cases have caused a backlash. These horrific stories of children raped and/or murdered have accentuated the number of child abuse reports.

- 160,000 reports of suspected child abuse were reported in 1963. That number exploded to 1.7 million in 1985.

- And a report disseminated by the National Center on Child Abuse and Neglect (NCCAN) [titled] *Child Maltreatment 1995: Reports From the States to the National Child Abuse and Neglect Data System,* depicts more than three million reports of alleged child abuse and neglect that year. However, two million of those complaints were without foundation or false!

In addition, our child protection laws . . . have instigated and invited scores of anonymous and unfounded reports of abuse to be made.

We will not win the war against child abuse until we first win the battle against false accusations.

Doctors Can Misdiagnose Child Abuse

Celeste Biever

Celeste Biever is a staff writer for New Scientist, *a British periodical.*

When Christina Nguyen-Phuoc's 12-day-old son suddenly refused to eat, became unresponsive and breathless, she took him to a hospital in Houston. X-rays revealed haemorrhages in his brain and eyes. Child protection services promptly put both her sons in care and took her to court.

"I told them that Andrew got sick overnight, and they said that that can't happen, you have to shake a baby to get a brain haemorrhage," Nguyen-Phuoc told *New Scientist.* Two months later, doctors discovered that her son actually had a rare blood disease called haemophagocytic lymphohistiocytosis (HLH).

This is one of three cases highlighted in a study in [a 2003] issue of *Pediatrics.* It is the first time attention has been drawn to the potential confusion between HLH and child abuse injuries. No one knows how many other cases there are like this worldwide—and the tragedy is not just that parents are wrongly accused, but that without prompt diagnosis and treatment HLH can be fatal.

Doctors Lack Awareness

The disease, which can be genetic or caused by infections such as glandular fever, is thought to affect just 1 in 50,000 babies. But many cases may be slipping through the net because of the lack of awareness among doctors, the absence of a quick-and-easy test for the disease and the fact that the link between brain symptoms and HLH was discovered only recently.

Celeste Biever, "It's Not Always Child Abuse," *New Scientist*, vol. 178, June 7, 2003, p. 4. Copyright © 2003 Reed Elsevier Business Publishing, Ltd. Reproduced by permisson.

The rareness of HLH and the commonness of child abuse are a disastrous combination. "Most paediatricians will never see a case of this during their careers," says James Whitlock of Vanderbilt College of Medicine in Nashville, Tennessee. So when they are confronted with symptoms such as retinal haemorrhaging, widely taken to be a sure sign of "inflicted injury," the logical assumption is child abuse.

Most of the time they are right. Indeed, child protection workers worry that raising the profile of HLH could let child abusers off the hook. "Child abuse is by far and away more common than HLH," says Jeanine Graf, a paediatrician and member of the child protection service at the Texas Children's Hospital in Houston, to which Nguyen-Phuoc's case was referred. She points out that three million children are abused each year in the US, whereas just 200 are known to suffer from HLH.

Recent Discoveries

This is a danger, agrees Kenneth McClain of the Baylor College of Medicine in Houston, one of the study's authors. But he hopes that strict adherence to the medical diagnosis of HLH will prevent lawyers twisting the disease to their advantage.

HLH is caused when disease-fighting cells called lymphocytes and macrophages fail to commit suicide when they are no longer needed. Instead, they attack normal cells and inhibit essential processes such as the production of blood platelets.

Only an autopsy can clearly distinguish between the brain damage caused by macrophages and that resulting from abuse.

The disease has long been known to disrupt liver and bone marrow function, but it was only recently discovered that it can also cause bleeding in the brain and eyes. It is these little-recognised symptoms that most closely resemble the tearing and bleeding inflicted by sudden movements of the head and neck, says Graf. A baby need not be shaken very hard to cause brain lesions.

It was the brain damage that convinced the child protection services in Nguyen-Phuoc's case. "They had a neurologist with thirty years' experience testify that he was 100 per cent sure that it was shaken-baby syndrome. It was all based on the X-rays," Nguyen-Phuoc says.

No Easy Tests

Only an autopsy can clearly distinguish between the brain damage caused by macrophages and that resulting from abuse. But if a child has HLH it strongly suggests that abuse is not to blame. Unfortunately, there is no easy way to diagnose the disease. The quick tests are inconclusive because the results overlap with those seen for other diseases such as hepatitis, encephalitis, sepsis and leishmaniasis. A test for lowered levels of "natural killer cells" in the blood is a sure sign of HLH, but it takes at least a week to get results.

"One of the most frustrating things about HLH is there is no widely available rapid test that will say yes or no," says Whitlock. But because HLH is rare, it is not a priority for research institutions.

Nguyen-Phuoc was lucky. Other doctors suspected HLH, the charges against her were dropped and her son was given a bone marrow transplant. The babies in the two other cases died, and the bereaved parents of one remain under suspicion because the hospital involved still refuses to accept that HLH can cause brain damage, despite McClain's efforts to persuade doctors there.

The Extent of Internet Child Pornography Has Been Exaggerated

Computer Crime Research Center

The Computer Crime Research Center is a nonprofit, nongovernmental scientific research organization based in Ukraine.

The hounding that has driven many suspects to suicide is based on tainted internet evidence, says expert witness Duncan Campbell. Ministers [government officials] . . . have announced plans to create a central database of internet paedophiles. Such a database would necessarily include the names of those convicted as part of Operation Ore, the huge police investigation launched [in 2002] on the basis of a list of 7,200 names supplied to British police forces by American colleagues.

Innocent People Are Falsely Accused of Viewing Child Porn

The men on the list are accused of having paid for child porn through Landslide, a website that operated in Texas from 1996–9. So far, about 1,200 cases have resulted in convictions. The public has been led to believe that a huge number of un-savoury—and possibly dangerous—men have been brought to book [arrested].

There is no dispute that abusing children is a hideous crime. But it is also appalling to be accused unjustly of such a crime. [Campbell's investigations and work as an expert witness in a number of Operation Ore cases have led [him] to believe that the evidence has been exaggerated and used unacceptably.]

Computer Crime Research Center, "A Flaw in the Child Porn Witch Hunt," www.crime research.org. Originally published in the Sunday Times, 26 June 2005. Reproduced by permission of the author.

The costs—in every sense—have been huge. Thousands of cases have been investigated, with scores of officers spending hundreds of weeks sifting through computers and disks. Thousands more may face investigation. Meanwhile, the accusations have led to 33 suicides, most recently that of Royal Navy Commodore David White, the commander of British forces in Gibraltar. On January 8, [2005] he was found dead in his pool.

Ministers appear not to have been informed that critical evidence from U.S. investigators forming the backbone of Operation Ore has been found to be untrue. In information given to Interpol and in sworn statements submitted to British courts in 2002, Dallas detective Steven Nelson and U.S. postal inspector Michael Mead claimed that everyone who went to Landslide always saw only a front page screen button offering "Click Here (for) Child Porn."

According to them, this was the way in to nearly 400 pay-per-view websites, almost all of which specialised in child pornography; ergo, anyone who accessed Landslide and paid it money must be a paedophile.

Many arrested [child porn] suspects who were cleared because there was no evidence . . . found their names and details leaked to the press.

Police Rely on Myths to Make Arrests

When Operation Ore was launched in Britain in May 2002, pictures of the web page and its "click here" button were given prominent and sustained publicity. But what passed almost unnoticed eight months later was that after British police and computer investigators had finally examined American files, they found that the "child porn" button was not on the front page of Landslide at all, but was an advertisement for another site appearing elsewhere: thus the crucial "child porn" button was a myth. . . .

Landslide operated two services, one of which gave access to thousands of sites for a small monthly fee. The other, called Keyz, was more expensive and required a separate payment for each site. The American investigators, it transpired, had copied the contents of 12 sites out of nearly 400 accessible through Keyz. Those sites definitely did contain child porn. It was also suspected that about a quarter of the other sites contained child porn. But investigations carried out more than a year after Operation Ore was launched found that about 180 Keyz sites were likely to have been adult sites only or were completely unknown. "We are unable to say what material these sites ever contained," a police report stated.

Authorities Pursue Unsubstantiated Cases

This was not a problem in early cases, which relied on actual possession of indecent images. But the length of time since the alleged offenses occurred—Landslide shut in 1999—meant that in many cases, there were no indecent images, just the record of name and credit card details.

Here, the American evidence that having paid to get into Landslide meant having paid to access child porn has become crucial. Many of the accused argue that their card details could have been stolen and used without their knowledge, or admit that they used Landslide, but for adult material. . . .

Even for those never charged, or acquitted before trial, the experiences are so scarring that very few want to talk.

Innocent People Become Targets

One of the targets was Robert Del Naja, frontman of the group Massive Attack, who was arrested in February 2003. All his computer equipment was seized. The case was dropped barely a month later. After being falsely arrested on child porn charges, Del Naja later described 2003 as the worst year of his life. "When the story was leaked to newspapers the human cost was horrible for me, my friends and family," he said.

Many arrested Operation Ore suspects who were cleared because there was no evidence also found their names and details leaked to the press. Information about Del Naja was leaked to *The Sun* [a London tabloid] before investigations concluded. The same thing happened to Who guitarist Pete Townshend, who later admitted visiting child porn sites as part of a research project. *The [London] Sunday Times* saw a complete copy of the Landslide British database of 7,200 names in January 2003. . . .

More False Cases

In April 2003, at the start of a Canadian investigation, Operation Snowball, Toronto police chief Julian Fantino held a high-profile press conference to announce arrests for child pornography. He publicly listed the names and ages of six men: one was never charged and three others later had all charges withdrawn.

One of those was James LeCraw, the director of a non-profit agency in Toronto providing computers to schools. He was suspended and later lost his job. But five months after the press conference, LeCraw was formally cleared. It was too late. Stigmatised, he killed himself on July 19, 2004.

A Scarring Experience

Even for those never charged, or acquitted before trial, the experiences are so scarring that very few want to talk. An exception is David Stanley, who runs his own computer-programming company in Wales. Like many men, from time to time he signed up for adult images on the net. In the summer of 1999 he saw his credit card details had been used five times in less than three weeks on the Landslide website. He complained quickly and got a refund. He thought no more of it until the police knocked on his door three years later.

Being an Operation Ore suspect was, he said, "a trial of the mind. I lost mine at the time. If people are guilty, they can say to themselves, yes, been there, done that. But if you haven't, then it's impossible to make sense of what's happening to your life." When Stanley proved to police that details he'd given for adult access had been stolen and reused at Landslide to send money to child porn merchants, his innocence was accepted.

Costly Mistakes

The laudable objective of Operation Ore was the protection of vulnerable children from adult abuse and harm. But many fear that mistakes have caused huge quantities of police, technical and social work resources to be misdirected to some futile and ill-founded investigations. Many families as well as accused men have been damaged, sometimes irretrievably, by the nature of the investigations. The claims made by the authorities may need to be weighed against the harm done to innocent lives.

Most Priests Do Not Abuse Children

B. A. Robinson

B. A. Robinson is the coordinator and writer for Ontario Consultants on Religious Tolerance.

Sexual abuse of youths and children in the U.S. by Roman Catholic priests has been quietly discussed for decades. A series of books on the topic was published starting during the 1990s and continuing today. But it was only in early 2002 that a moral panic surfaced, alleging widespread child and youth sexual abuse by priests. The little data that is available seems to indicate that the abusers represent a very small percentage of the total priesthood. Further, very few of those priests who do abuse are actually pedophiles, as the media often reports. Rather they are hebephiles—adult priests with a homosexual or bisexual orientation, and who are also sexually attracted to post-pubertal males. Their victims are teenage males who are under the age of 18. . . .

Media Reports Are Often Inaccurate

During the first few months of 2002, revelations of pedophilia, ephebophilia and hebephilia among some priests in the Roman Catholic church spread like wildfire across the U.S. The media gave the impression that:

> *Most of the abusing priests were pedophiles—molesting little children.* Actually, most of the criminal acts were by hebephiles—engaging in sexual activity with post-pubertal, 13- to 17-year-old young men.

> *Many priests abuse children.* Actually, the vast majority of Roman Catholic clergy are either celibate, or married, or

B. A. Robinson, "What Percentage of Priests Abuse, and Whom do They Victimize?" www.religioustolerance.org/clergy_sex8.htm, April 25, 2005. Reproduced by permission of Ontario Consultants on Religious Tolerance.

discreetly engaged in sexual behavior with other adults. There is general agreement that only a [small] percentage of the clergy actually abuse children sexually. The U.S. Conference of Catholic Bishops released a national study in 2004-February which concluded that about 4% of all U.S. priests since 1950 have been accused of sexual abuse of children. However, there are probably many victims who have remained silent and not come forward to accuse their abuser(s).

There are probably many adults who have come forward to accuse priests, who have false recovered memories of abuse that never happened.

There may be some adults who knowingly falsely accuse innocent priests of abuse in order to collect compensation.

A massive amount of abuse is now going on in the Roman Catholic church. The data that appear in the media often reflects allegations of abuse which have accumulated over the past forty years. The number of cases involving allegations of recent abuse will be a small fraction of the total that is now being reported.

Priests abuse at a per-capita rate that is much greater than for the general population. This is probably true, even if for no other reason that all Roman Catholic priests are currently male, and adult males have a much higher abuse rate than females. . . .

Accurate Data Is Difficult to Obtain

Frederick S. Berlin is the director of the National Institute for the Study, Prevention and Treatment of Sexual Trauma, and a widely published author on sexual disorders. He stated in an interview: "There is no good data either from the general population or from the priesthood about numbers of pedophiles or people who have a vulnerability that increases their risk to children. The issue of sexuality, particularly of people who may have unusual kinds of sexual cravings, has been one that society has tended to sweep under the carpet. Getting that data is terribly important, but as of now I know of no systematic surveys that would allow us to come to any firm conclusions." . . .

Most Priests Are Not Abusers

Philip Jenkins is a professor of history and religious studies at Penn State University and has written a book on the topic. He estimates that 2% of priests sexually abuse youth and children.

Richard Sipe is a psychotherapist and former priest, who has studied celibacy and sexuality in the priesthood for four decades. He has authored three books on the topic. By extrapolating from his 25 years of interviews of 1,500 priests and others, he estimates that 6% of priests abuse. Of these, 4% abuse teens, aged 13 to 17; 2% abuse pre-pubertal children.

The general consensus is that the vast majority of priests do not abuse young people.

Sylvia M. Demarest, a lawyer from Texas, has been tracking accusations against priests since the the mid-1990s. By 1996, she had identified 1,100 priests who had been accused of molesting children. She predicts that when she updates the list, the total will exceed 1,500 names. This represents about 2.5% of the approximately 60,000 men who have been active priests in the U.S. since 1984. It is important to realize that these are accused priests; the allegations have not been evaluated in a trial. Also, there is no way to judge what proportion of abusive priests are on her list. It may include 40% or fewer; she may have found 90% or more.

Columnist Ann Coulter claimed, without citing references, that there are only 55 "exposed abusers" in a population of 45,000 priests. This is an abuse rate of 0.12%. . . .

It is important to keep one's eye on the forest and not on the trees. Even if, as one researcher estimates, six percent of priests sexually abuse youth or children, then that still leaves an average of almost 19 priests out of every 20 who are non-abusive. . . .

A Portrait of the Abusers

The general consensus is that the vast majority of priests do not abuse young people. Among those who do, most fall within the following definitions:

> Abusive pedophiles who have a heterosexual orientation and are sexually attracted to pre-pubertal girls, less commonly to boys, and sometimes to both boys and girls. They often have sexual feelings to children of a particular age group—e.g. 7 and 8 year olds.

> Abusive hebephiles (a.k.a. ephebophiles) who are priests with a homosexual orientation. They are sexually attracted to post-pubertal young men, aged 13 to 17 years. Most are also probably attracted to adult males.

Nobody knows, with any degree of accuracy, what percentage of priests fall into each category. . . .

Donald Cozzens, former vicar of priests at the Diocese of Cleveland, OH, wrote in the year 2000 about his experience in the Midwest: "As a group, [child sexual] abusers tend to be married men who prey on girls, although many pedophiles abuse both girls and boys. Our respective diocesan experience revealed that roughly 90 percent of priest abusers targeted teenage boys as their victims. . . . Relatively little attention has been paid to this phenomenon by church authorities. Perhaps it is feared that it will call attention to the disproportionate number of gay priests. While homosexually oriented people are no more likely to be drawn to misconduct with minors than straight people, our own experience was clear and, I believe, significant. Most priest offenders, we vicars agreed, acted out against teenage boys." . . .

Age of Consent Variations Affect the Statistics

It is worth noting that if the age of consent for homosexual activity were lowered to the age of 16, as it is in many jurisdictions, then most of the criminal acts by abusive priests would disappear. Most charges by the police against abusive priests would disappear. Cases of hebephilia would still represent an ethical quagmire, however. They would be a gross violation of the priest's ordination vows and would be an extremely harmful experience to most of the teens. . . .

Better Training for Priests Is Needed

Bishop Thomas Gumbelton of Detroit has said that, in the past, Catholic seminaries had not adequately prepared students for a lifetime of celibacy. They had not taught students how to integrate their sexuality.

Barbara Walters of ABC's *20/20* has stated that ". . .the [Catholic] church has made dramatic changes in the last decade in the way it addresses sexual issues in seminary. Instead of denying or repressing sexual desire, seminaries now use progressive psychology to help men deal openly with the once taboo topics of sexual attraction as well as homosexuality. Seminarians, for example, learn how to channel their sexual energy, and that it is alright to embrace their homosexual orientation. They are taught that intimate, nonsexual friendships may help keep them from breaking their vow of celibacy."

It will take decades to determine the effectiveness of these sex-ed programs in preventing sexual abuse.

CHAPTER 2

What Factors Contribute to Child Abuse?

Overview: The Factors That Contribute to Child Abuse

Mei Ling Rein

Mei Ling Rein is a freelance writer and editor.

Raising a child is not easy. Everyday stresses, strains, and sporadic upheavals in family life, coupled with the normal burdens of child care, cause most parents to feel angry at times. People who would not dream of hitting a colleague or an acquaintance when they are angry may think nothing of hitting their children. Some feel remorse after hitting a loved one; nevertheless, when they are angry, they still resort to violence. The deeper intimacy and greater commitment in a family make emotionally charged disagreements more frequent and more intense. . . .

Some Contributing Factors to Child Abuse

The factors contributing to child maltreatment are complex. The *Third National Incidence Study of Child Abuse and Neglect* (NIS-3) . . . found that family structure and size, poverty, alcohol and substance abuse, domestic violence, and community violence are contributing factors to child abuse and neglect. . . .

[Researchers] Murray A. Straus and Christine Smith noted, in "Family Patterns and Child Abuse," that one cannot simply single out an individual factor as the cause of abuse. The authors found that a combination of several factors is more likely to result in child abuse than is a single factor by itself. Also, the sum of the effects of individual factors taken together does not necessarily add up to what Straus and Smith called the "explosive combinations" of several factors interacting with one another. Nonetheless, even "explosive combinations" do not necessarily lead to child abuse.

Mei Ling Rein, "Child Abuse: Betraying a Trust," Farmington Hills, MI: Information Plus Reference Series, 2005. Reproduced by permission of Thomson Gale.

Poverty and Abuse

/Although the most comprehensive U.S. government report on the incidence of child maltreatment, NIS-3, found a correlation between family income and child abuse and neglect, most experts agree that the connection between poverty and maltreatment is not easily explained. According to Diana J. English, the stress that comes with poverty may predispose the parents to use corporal punishment that may lead to physical abuse.\

English noted that most poor parents do not maltreat their children. Rather, the effects of poverty, such as stress, may influence other risk factors, including depression, substance abuse, and domestic violence. These risk factors, in turn, may predispose the parents to violent behavior toward their children.

There are no 'vacations' from being a parent, and parenting stress has been associated with abusive behavior.

According to the National Center for Children in Poverty (NCCP), research has shown that the problems of depression, substance abuse, and domestic violence are interrelated and that these problems are more likely to be prevalent among low-income families. NCCP noted that federally funded and community-based programs, such as Early Head Start, designed to help low-income parents and their infants and toddlers, recognize the connection between poverty and parental and child well-being.

The 1975 National Family Violence Survey found rates of child abuse that were considerably higher among families suffering from unemployment than among those in which the husband was working full time. Families in which the husband was not working had a significantly higher rate of child abuse than other families (22.5 versus 13.9 per one hundred children). This finding did not recur, however, in the 1985 survey, although wives of unemployed husbands did have a higher rate of abuse than wives of husbands working full time (16.2 versus eleven per one hundred children). Straus and Smith ("Family Patterns and Child Abuse") thought that this higher rate for wives might have been caused by added family stress because the father was unemployed. . . .

The rate of abuse in the 1985 *National Family Violence Resurvey* was considerably higher in families in which the husband was a blue-collar worker. Blue-collar fathers committed abuse at a rate of 11.9 per 100 children, compared with 8.9 per 100 children among white-collar workers. . . .

Stress Contributes to Child Abuse

There are no "vacations" from being a parent, and parenting stress has been associated with abusive behavior. When a parent who may be predisposed toward maltreating a child must deal with a particularly stressful situation, it is possible that little time, energy, or self-control is left for the children. In times of stress, the slightest action by the child can be "the last straw" that leads to violent abuse.

[Often, when striking out at a child, the parent may be venting anger at his or her own situation rather than reacting to some misbehavior on the part of the child.] Abused children have indicated that they never knew when their parents' anger would explode and that they were severely beaten for the most minor infractions. The child may also be hostile and aggressive, contributing to the stress.

Caring for Children with Disabilities

Children with disabilities are potentially at risk for maltreatment because society generally treats them as different and less valuable, thus possibly tolerating violence against them. These children require special care and attention, and parents may not have the social support to help ease stressful situations. A lack of financial resources further exacerbates the situation.

Some parents may feel disappointment at not having a "normal" child. Others may expect too much and feel frustrated if the child does not live up to their expectations. Children under the care of nonfamily members are at risk for maltreatment, not only from those caregivers who abuse their power or who feel no bond with them, but also from other children, especially in an institutional setting. . . .

[One] study . . . found a 64% prevalence rate of maltreatment among disabled children.

Children with disabilities may also be vulnerable to sexual abuse. Dependent on caregivers for their physical needs, these children may not be able to distinguish between appropriate and inappropriate touching of their bodies. The opportunities for sexual abuse may also be increased if the child depends on several caregivers for his or her needs. . . . Children with disabilities may not be intellectually capable of understanding that they are being abused. They may not have the communication skills to disclose the abuse. In addition, children who experience some pain when undergoing therapy may not be able to distinguish between inflicted pain and therapy pain. . . .

[Researcher Patricia M.] Sullivan and her colleagues undertook two epidemiological studies on maltreated children with disabilities. (Epidemiological studies take into consideration individuals' sex, age, race, social class, and other demographics.) The incidence of maltreatment (the number of new cases during a given period, such as per week, per month, or per year) and its prevalence (the total number of maltreated children with disabilities at a given time) are then measured. The hospital-based study of six thousand abused children found a 64% prevalence rate of maltreatment among disabled children, twice the prevalence rate (32%) among nondisabled children. The school-based study included 4,954 children, of which 31% of disabled children had been maltreated, 3.4 times that of the nondisabled comparison group. . . .

Toilet Training Can Lead to Child Abuse

Toilet training can be one of the most frustrating events in the lives of parents and children. Researchers are now linking it to many of the more serious, even deadly, cases of abuse in children between the ages of one and four. Some parents have unrealistic expectations regarding bowel and bladder control for young children, and when their children are unable to live up to these standards, the parents explode in rage. Parental stress and inability to control emotions play a role in child abuse, but they require a trigger to set off the explosion. Soiled clothes and accidents frequently serve as this trigger.

Parents who verbally abuse their children are also more likely to physically abuse their children.

When children are brought to the emergency room with deep, symmetrical scald burns on their bottoms, health care personnel conclude that they were deliberately immersed and held in hot water. This form of abuse is nearly always committed as the result of a toilet accident. Even a one-second contact with 147°F water can cause third-degree burns. Some parents think that immersing a child in hot water will make the child go to the bathroom. . . .

Spousal Verbal Aggression and Child Abuse

Husbands and wives sometimes use verbal aggression to deal with their conflicts. The 1985 *National Family Violence Resurvey* found that spouses who verbally attacked each other were also more likely to abuse their children. Among verbally aggressive husbands, the child abuse rate was 11.2 per one hundred children, compared with 4.9 per one hundred children for other husbands. Verbally aggressive wives had a child abuse rate of 12.3 per one hundred children, compared with 5.3 per one hundred children for other wives. Straus and Smith believe that verbal attacks between spouses, rather than clearing the air, tended to both mask the reason for the dispute and create further conflict. The resulting additional tension made it even harder to resolve the original source of conflict.

Verbal Abuse of Children Increases the Likelihood of Physical Abuse

Parents who verbally abuse their children are also more likely to physically abuse their children. Respondents to the 1975 National Family Violence Survey who verbally abused their children reported a child abuse rate six times that of other parents (twenty-one versus 3.6 per one hundred children). The 1985 survey found that verbally abusive mothers physically abused their children about nine times more than other mothers (16.3 versus 1.8 per one hundred children). Fathers who were verbally aggressive toward their children physically abused the children more than three times as much as other fathers (14.3 versus 4.2 per one hundred children).

Spousal Physical Aggression and Child Abuse

In "Family Patterns and Child Abuse," Straus and Smith reported that one of the most distinct findings of the 1985 *National Family Violence Resurvey* was that violence in one family relationship is frequently associated with violence in other family relationships. In families in which the husband struck his wife, the child abuse rate was much higher (22.3 per one hundred children) than in other families (eight per one hundred children). Similarly, in families in which the wife hit the husband, the child abuse rate was also considerably higher (22.9 per one hundred children) than in families in which the wife did not hit the husband (9.2 per one hundred children).

In "Risk of Physical Abuse to Children of Spouse Abusing Parents" (*Child Abuse & Neglect*, vol. 20, no. 7, January 1996), Susan Ross, who did further research based on the 1985 *National Family Violence Resurvey*, reported that marital violence was a statistically significant predictor of physical child abuse. Ross noted that the probability of child abuse by a violent husband increased from 5% with one act of marital violence to near certainty with fifty or more acts of spousal abuse. The percentages were similar for violent wives.

Children . . . who suffered childhood abuse or neglect were more likely than those with no reported maltreatment to be arrested as juveniles.

Ross found that, of those husbands who had been violent with their wives, 22.8% had engaged in violence toward their children. Similarly, 23.9% of violent wives had engaged in at least one act of physical child abuse. These rates of child abuse were much higher than those of parents who were not violent toward each other (8.5% for fathers and 9.8% for mothers). In other words, the more frequent the spousal violence, the higher the probability of child abuse. . . .

The Cycle of Violence

[Researcher Cathy S.] Widom is widely known for her work on the "cycle of violence." The cycle of violence theory suggests that childhood physical abuse increases the likelihood of arrest and of committing violent crime during the victim's later years. Widom found that, although a large proportion of maltreated children did not become juvenile delinquents or criminals, those who suffered childhood abuse or neglect were more likely than those with no reported maltreatment to be arrested as juveniles (31.2% versus 19%) and as adults (48.4% versus 36.2%). The maltreated victims (21%) were also more likely than those with no reported childhood maltreatment history (15.6%) to be arrested for a violent crime during their teen years or adulthood. . . .

Parents who were physically punished . . . were three times as likely . . . to abuse their children physically.

Gender played a role in the development of psychological disorders in adolescence and adulthood. Females (24.3%) with a history of childhood maltreatment were more likely to attempt suicide, compared with their male counterparts (13.4%). A significantly larger percentage of male victims (27%), however, than female victims (9.8%) were at a higher risk for future antisocial personality disorder. Although both male maltreated (64.4%) and control (67%) subjects had similar proportions of alcohol abuse or dependence, females who experienced abuse or neglect were more likely than the control group to have alcohol problems (43.8% versus 32.8%). . . .

Corporal Punishment Increases the Risk of Physical Abuse

Murray A. Straus presented a model called "path analysis" to illustrate how physical punishment could escalate to physical abuse ("Physical Abuse," Chapter 6 in *Beating the Devil Out of Them: Corporal Punishment in American Families and Its Effects on Children*, 2nd ed., New Brunswick, NJ: Transaction Publishers, 2001). Straus theorized that parents who have been physically disciplined as adolescents are more likely to believe that it is acceptable to use violence to remedy a misbehavior. These parents tend to be depressed and to be involved in spousal violence. When a parent resorts to physical punishment and the child does not comply, the parent increases the severity of the punishment, eventually harming the child.

Corporal punishment experienced in adolescence produces the same effect on males and females. Parents who were physically punished thirty or more times as adolescents (24%) were three times as likely as those who never received physical punishment (7%) to abuse their children physically. . . .

Some Minority Cultural Practices Qualify as Child Abuse

Eleanor T. Campbell

Eleanor T. Campbell is an assistant professor of nursing at Lehman College of the City University of New York.

In many parts of the world, child abuse has only recently emerged as a major social problem. Media exposure of child sexual trafficking and employment of minors has heightened public awareness of child maltreatment as a global issue. The World Health Organization (WHO) and the United Nations have defined four areas of child abuse and neglect, including physical abuse, child sexual abuse, neglect and negligent treatment, and emotional abuse. The majority of countries of the world have accepted these definitions. However, implementation of these definitions to prevent child abuse varies among cultures. While governments and agencies define child abuse based on public policy, social and cultural acceptance is based on cultural context. For example, "the Vietnamese practice of 'coining,' (rubbing the chest [with a coin]), and 'cupping,' (placing heated cups over the chest of a child with respiratory illness), instead of using antibiotics and humidification has been seen as a form of child neglect and abuse by Western health care professionals."

Some Parenting Practices Conflict with the Law

The affinity one has for one's own cultural values and child-rearing practices sometimes conflicts with the legal definition of child abuse and neglect. Research indicates that adults par-

Eleanor T. Campbell, "Child Abuse Recognition, Reporting and Prevention: A Culturally Congruent Approach," *Journal of Multicultural Nursing & Health*, vol. 11, July 1, 2005. Copyright Riley Publications, Inc. Center for the Study of Multiculturalism and Heath, Summer 2005. Reproduced by permisson.

ent as they have been reared; this includes nurses and other mandated reporters of child abuse who view certain child care practices through their own set of experiential lenses based upon their own personal upbringing and set of cultural values. . . . As nurses and client populations become even more culturally diverse, preventing recognizing and reporting cases of suspected abuse present a growing concern.

Recent reports of child abuse indicate that there are three million cases nationally, with approximately one million confirmed. Tragically, averages of two thousand children die each year as a consequence of child abuse or neglect. In 2001 childhood fatalities were estimated at 1,200, or 1.71 children per 100,000 population of children. Findings of maltreatment are proportionately higher for children of ethnic minority groups.

Statistics on race and ethnicity of victims of child abuse indicate a higher percentage among certain minority children. Data based on percentages per thousand children are 21.7% for American Indian or Alaska Native, 20.2% for African Americans, 10.7% for Whites, 9.5% for Hispanics, and 3.7% for Asian/Pacific Islanders. Although reports of maltreatment are proportionately higher among minorities, determination of maltreatment is not consistent. Reasons for the increase in reports of abuse for minority children vary, however. Economic disparities account for a significant number among this population who are exposed to greater public scrutiny by social service organizations in comparison to middle class families. These findings indicate the need for cultural considerations both ethnic and socioeconomic in order to decrease the incidence of false accusations of child maltreatment by professionals and the devastating consequences to families of such reporting. . . .

There Is No Universal Definition of Child Abuse

Among certain economic and cultural/religious groups corporal punishment may be an accepted form of discipline. For example, parenting measures among Southern Baptists, including Whites and African Americans, and [among] Asian groups may be more authoritarian in nature, valuing unquestioning obedience to rules and standards. "Among Asian Americans, obedience and strictness rather than being associated with harshness and domination, have more to do with caring, concern, and involvement and with maintaining family harmony." Adults who were physically disciplined may be more likely to accept this practice as the normal and correct way to reinforce societal rules and values.

Comparative studies on discipline between middle class and lower socio-economic cultures indicate more permissive and authoritative parenting styles among middle class parents. It should be noted that most professionals are from the middle class but may vary in their pre-professional cultural value systems. . . .

Since there are no universal standards for child rearing, and what is considered neglect in one culture may not be considered abnormal in another, some experts suggest that several determinations should be made in culturally informed assessments based on the following questions [as listed by Perle S. Cowen]: "(a) Is the practice viewed as neglectful by cultures other than the one in question? (b) Does the practice represent an idiosyncratic departure from one's cultural practice? And (c) Does the practice represent culturally induced harm to children beyond the control of parents or caretakers?"

Culturally Congruent Care

Madeleine Leininger's Culture Care Diversity and Universality theory (2001) is an appropriate model to use when working with diverse cultures of both health seekers and health givers. Leininger's theory is the first nursing theory that includes cultural competence and caring, which she calls culturally congruent care. This culturally congruent care is achieved through cultural care preservation or maintenance, cultural care accommodation or negotiation and cultural care repatterning or restructuring of behaviors. Using this model the nurse acts as a liaison and advocate to bridge the gap between generic cultural practices and the professional care systems. The theory has served as a guide for nursing research and practice of various aspects of culture and caring of individuals, families, and groups. Further, it supports preservation of "risk absent" or non-harmful behaviors that are part of traditional lifestyles while incorporating professional care systems that are congruent with these practices.

Leininger's theory examines the worldview or social/ cultural dimensions of a group of people from their perspective using informants (community leaders) within a particular cultural group. Investigation of political, social, economic, religious, and educational factors influencing the care expressions, patterns and practices are a part of the cultural assessment needed to fully understand the culture prior to planning and intervening in the care of a particular group. Nurses are at the center of coordinating professional care systems and cultural or folk systems to provide culturally congruent care.

Assisting caretakers with learning new ways of doing and modifying their actions to achieve better outcomes for the child's behavior or health is the goal of this model as applied to this situation. Folk ways that both support cultural values and achieve the intended goal can be determined and supported by both the caretaker and the professional nurse. Likewise generic practices that are harmful to the child would be repatterned to achieve the best outcome for the child without eroding cultural integrity. Assessment of family roles and organization within specific cultures would be significant to understanding the traditions of diverse populations in terms of child care and discipline. Viewing suspected maltreatment cases within context is necessary for accurate interpretation. The following case example is offered to help clarify assessment and evaluation of suspected child maltreatment. CAPTA [Child Abuse Prevention and Treatment Act] criteria for defining child maltreatment are used to identify child neglect. Leininger's theoretical model is used to repattern or restructure harmful behaviors while maintaining values and non-harmful cultural practices of childcare.

A Sample Case

The community health nurse in a large urban region makes a home visit to a family to assess the health maintenance of an infant child recently discharged from the hospital with a chronic respiratory condition. Knocking on the apartment door, the nurse hears the voices of young children and inquires as to the whereabouts of the parents. The children state that their mother is not at home. Within a few minutes the mother appears from outside. She has gone to the corner store leaving her four- and five-year-old children alone with the eight-month-old infant patient. The family is from a small village in Nigeria, and many of the apartment residents are also Nigerian. It is customary for people from this village in West Africa to look after the welfare of their neighbors. The nurse is aware of these cultural dimensions yet determines that in a large urban setting unsupervised young children are vulnerable to injury and accidents. A report to Child Protective Services (CPS) is made and the family is investigated by a caseworker for suspected child neglect.

According to state laws in this jurisdiction a capable adult must directly supervise young children. Although the infant and other children were unharmed, the potential for such harm in this case is great and left unreported such parental behavior would most likely continue based upon traditional beliefs and practices in the homeland. The nurse is correct in initiating a report. Failure to make a report would not only be unethical and unprofessional, this behavior would be considered legally negligent. The nurse could be liable both civilly and criminally for any harm coming to the children as a result of failure to initiate a report. Under state law, protective immunity or protection from retaliatory liability by the parents against the nurse and caseworker is given due to good-faith reporting. The nurse's report to the caseworker and Child Protective Services was made to protect the children and to prevent harm, not as a punitive measure against the mother.

After investigation by CPS and appearance in Family Court the decision is to keep the children in the home since no physical or emotional harm has been done to the children. The family is to receive follow-up home visits by another community health nurse to teach the parents appropriate child safety principles, to aid the family in adjusting to child rearing in the new urban setting, and to reinforce the local child welfare laws in relation to parental responsibility.

Implementing a global standard of child maltreatment . . . continues to be a dilemma due to the high level of cultural diversity,

---

The home care nurse makes a visit to the family and assesses the environment and the family interaction using guidelines from community health nursing literature. The nurse finds the two-bedroom apartment to be small but clean, neat, and free of vermin. The family of five includes the father who works outside of the home, the mother who is the primary homemaker and three children, ages five and four years and eight months. The infant patient is asleep in a crib in his room that is shared with two other siblings. Each child has her own bed in this small room. There are window guards on all windows and a smoke alarm detector as legally required for safety. Age appropriate toys are about the living room where the children have been playing. During the nurse's physical assessment of the infant the siblings interact appropriately by observing quietly. The mother bonds well with the infant by holding and calling the child by name. She is knowledgeable of the infant's prescribed medication's route, dose and storage away from the younger siblings. The nurse reinforces the safe storage of the medication.

During the visit a neighbor from upstairs comes down to talk with the mother. The visitor is another Nigerian woman from the family's village. She baby-sits the children when the mother takes the infant for clinic appointments. The nurse recommends that this person also be asked to supervise the children when the mother needs to shop and leave the apartment so that the children are never left unattended by an adult. Since the home is equipped with a telephone this could be done without the mother leaving her apartment. This is an example of cultural repatterning or using existing behavior of the community involvement in childcare with the neighbor to prevent the potential for "child abandonment" issues and reports of child neglect in the future. The nurse will continue to make follow-up visits to this family to reinforce principles of normal child development and safety and well-child care and to evaluate the infant's respiratory status. The mother is receptive to these visits and understands that they are a part of the Family Court decision and health care follow-up for the infant. She also understands that leaving the children unattended could be potentially harmful and has a viable plan to contact her neighbor for baby-sitting needs in the future.

Implementing a global standard of child maltreatment that is useful in guiding professionals to recognize and prevent child abuse while supporting culture-bound child-rearing practices continues to be a dilemma due to the high level of cultural diversity. Problems of misinterpretation of parenting behaviors and clinical findings of maltreatment exist despite legal guidelines from international, national and regional authorities. Reasons for possible misinterpretations range from ignorance of cultural norms and practices to professional culture-bound belief systems and practices.

Methamphetamine Labs Can Lead to Child Endangerment

Jerry Harris

Jerry Harris heads the training and education section of the Oklahoma Bureau of Narcotics and Dangerous Drugs Control in Oklahoma City, Oklahoma.

The number of children in the United States exposed to the inherently hazardous processes used in the illicit manufacture of the controlled dangerous substance methamphetamine, or meth, has more than doubled in the past few years. Unfortunately, despite law enforcement efforts, these numbers continue to rise.

Just as alarming is the number of children negatively impacted by physical and emotional abuse, as well as neglect, by parents, guardians, or other adults who expose them to toxic meth lab operations, firearms, pornographic material, criminals and their unlawful activity, and domestic violence, just to name a few of the dangers. Methamphetamine abuse and production have become major factors in the increase of child abuse and neglect cases handled by the child welfare system.

The Growing Menace

Estimates have indicated that children are found in approximately one-third of all seized meth labs. Of those children, about 35 percent test positive for toxic levels of chemicals in their bodies. In other areas, those numbers have proven even higher. More alarming, however, is the possibility that 90 percent of all meth labs go undetected, leaving many children to suffer needlessly.

Although statistics are limited at present, an abundance of anecdotal evidence exists about the enormous physical, developmental, emotional, and psychosocial damage suffered by children exposed to illegal home-based drug production. The evidence comes from professionals in the fields of law enforcement, human services, medicine, education, and others who have first-hand experience with children living in homes where methamphetamine is illegally manufactured.

Children who inhabit homes where parents, guardians, or other adults undertake the illegal manufacturing of methamphetamine risk multiple exposures to many different chemicals and combinations of chemicals and their byproducts. They further risk toxic poisoning from the inhalation of chemical gases and vapors that damage their respiratory and circulatory systems; chemical burns; and the ingestion, absorption, or injection of drugs or chemicals. Such children also face the peril of injury or death from fires or explosions.

The [meth-lab-operating] parents . . . have been getting away with the abuse and neglect of their children for a long time.

Often, these children live in poor conditions. Homes that house labs frequently are dirty, sometimes lacking water, heat, and electricity. The children typically have little to eat and do not receive adequate medical care, including immunizations, and dental services. The mothers rarely seek prenatal care for some of the same exposures. This constitutes not only child endangerment but, even worse, child abuse.

Exposure to these dangerous substances can cause serious short- and long-term health problems, including damage to the brain, liver, kidneys, lungs, eyes, and skin. The chaotic lifestyle of individuals involved in methamphetamine manufacturing and use places children at risk for physical and emotional trauma. To compound the problem, neglect or inconsistent parenting can interfere with children's cognitive, emotional, and social development. The children become exposed to drug-related violence and physical and sexual abuse at the hands of family members, neighbors, and an array of strangers who pass through the house to buy or sell drugs.

Relatively few states have programs in place to deal with the problems associated with the manufacture of methamphetamine, especially when it comes to the children caught up in this illegal activity. The social and legal aspects of these types of cases are enormous. The parents, more often than not, have been getting away with the abuse and neglect of their children for a long time. The children found at these meth lab sites have suffered greatly and been denied access to social and health-related services. What can be done to protect these drug-endangered children?

First responders must recognize that intervention on behalf of these children is of the utmost importance.

Oklahoma's Response

In Oklahoma, a program began operating ad hoc after months of preparation and training. Meetings involved representatives from social, medical, law enforcement, and criminal justice agencies. These professionals saw the need and, thus, conjointly formed a state drug-endangered children (DEC) effort that, so far, has attempted to mirror the DEC program in California.

The goal of the DEC effort is to intervene on behalf of children found living in horrific conditions produced by the unlawful and dangerous clandestine methamphetamine manufacturing processes and the environment associated with addiction. A further goal involves creating a collaborative multidisciplinary community response to identify and meet the short- and long-term needs of the children endangered by this exposure.

To accomplish this goal, the DEC program steering committee was set up to offer assistance to the multidisciplinary child abuse and neglect teams (CAN) that Oklahoma has mandated every county to establish. Currently, there are 50 functional teams, with more forming. The CAN teams, comprised of law enforcement officers, child protective service workers, mental health employees, medical personnel, prosecutors, and other professionals, address problems of child abuse and neglect and currently are the best suited to respond to the needs of drug-endangered children. Many teams, who have been called upon to do so, have worked in concert with other professionals to see that these children receive the kind of short- and long-term care needed and, when appropriate, ensure that the violators are prosecuted for child endangerment.

Collaboration Is Needed for Success

Only by working collaboratively can these professionals succeed in their endeavors. They must work toward a "win-win" situation in the best interest of the children. First responders must recognize that intervention on behalf of these children is of the utmost importance. This intervention, however, must take place without creating additional trauma to the children. Law enforcement officers take the children into protective custody, move them to a safe location, and attend to their immediate needs. Child protective services (CPS) personnel arrive on the scene as soon as possible to help the officers assess the needs of the children. Emergency medical technicians (EMTs), firefighters, and hazardous material professionals also stand by if needed.

Such coordinated efforts prove invaluable to the well-being of the children and must be worked out in advance and included in the operational protocols of the CAN team. For example, because removal of clothes and decontamination procedures according to federal instructions are certain to cause an increased sense of vulnerability and trauma to all but the smallest infants, this only should occur prior to CPS arrival in the most pressing and urgent circumstances.

While the presence of toxins . . . support child abuse charges, it is most important as a possible indicator of other chemical exposures and for identifying and treating any adverse health effects.

The children should be transported to the appropriate medical screening facility for further evaluation as soon as possible after the intervention. If grossly contaminated children are discovered, they should be examined on the scene by trained EMTs. The children then should be transported by ambulance just in case complications arise en route. EMTs also should consider that they are traveling in a confined space and should allow for ventilation.

Determining which member of the team should transport the children proves crucial to the CAN team's effectiveness. In the best interest of the children, team members must agree on the most appropriate method of transporting them. In some cases, a CPS worker may be the best choice. CAN members must consider the children's ages, as well as the safety of the person providing the transportation. While officers must maintain control of the situation, they may encounter difficulties in transporting the children to a medical screening facility out of their jurisdiction. The number of officers on duty may dictate whether they can leave their jurisdiction for that purpose. When officers provide the transportation, they cannot remain with the children at the medical screening facility for any length of time, no matter how much they would wish to, because they must return to their official duties. Similarly, the

CAN team also must coordinate transportation to the receiving facility. The vast majority of the children taken into protective custody are eventually placed with relatives, while the remainder are sent to shelters.

Courts Play a Vital Role

Having a standing court order from the jurisdictional judge when children are found in meth labs expedites assuming temporary custody for the CPS worker. A standing court order regarding toxicology testing also helps in testing for ingested or assimilated chemicals and drugs. Based on the results of a urinalysis test, a blood test may be warranted and in the best interest of the children's health in terms of follow-up care. Although it is strongly recommended that children's urine/blood be obtained if possible within 2 hours as part of evidence collection, this is not absolutely necessary to conduct a thorough DEC investigation or prosecution. While the presence of toxins in the child's urine or blood will support child abuse charges, it is most important as a possible indicator of other chemical exposures and for identifying and treating any adverse health effects.

Based on the California Drug-Endangered Children Program and what Oklahoma authorities have seen thus far, an effective comprehensive response to the needs of children endangered by the epidemic of methamphetamine use and production, as well as all substance abuse, must include prevention, intervention, enforcement, interdiction, and treatment. Multidisciplinary collaboration is key to ensuring that this comprehensive range of responses is activated.

Religion Can Inspire Child Abuse

Narisetti Innaiah

Narisetti Innaiah is vice president of the Rationlist Association of India and a national executive member of the Indian Radical Humanist Association. He has published books and articles in English and Telugu on politics, philosophy, skepticism, and humanism.

"Our children are our own. They are ours to thrash or kill, if we choose; who are you to poke your nose in?" Yes, millions of parents still feel that way, in every part of the world. They justify harsh punishments with dictums like "You can train a plant but not a tree," or "Spare the rod and spoil the child." Too many traditional religions encourage parents to regard children as their property—or to believe that the more children they have, the better. "A child has not only a mouth but also two earning hands." Where do sayings like these come from? Which social institutions underlie much of the child abuse endemic to the world today, yet are scarcely ever accused by name? Religions, of course. It is religions that inspire and perpetuate much of the abuse that afflicts children around the globe.

The Power of Religion

Over the ages, religions have exploited the power of the bond between parents and children, fashioning priestly infrastructures that touch every aspect of life, enmeshing families ever deeper in allegiance. In most cultures this entrapment begins at or soon after birth with the naming of the baby. Parents feel it their duty to abide by religious customs, traditions and rituals. This, in turn, assures a livelihood to the priestly class.

Narisetti Innaiah, "Child Abuse by Religions," *Free Inquiry*, vol. 23, July 1, 2003. Copyright 2003 Council for Secular Humanism, Inc. Reproduced by permission.

Priests encourage parents to bring their children along when they visit places of worship. Parents obey, often hoping that experiences in the temple, church, mosque, or synagogue will help children develop faith in God and to practice ethical conduct. Children are thus controlled right from birth, in all countries and in all religions. Believing parents do not merely indoctrinate their children on the virtues of their own religion. They warn their young against embracing other religions, against following their customs and beliefs. Thus are the seeds of hatred sown, directly or indirectly, in impressionable minds.

When religion and science conflict, most people follow religion and give science a pass.

Children are not born into religion; of necessity, they are born not even knowing what religion is. Yet, the religion of their parents is attributed to them. By the time they start talking, then writing, they can name their religion because it has been named for them. Thus steeped in religion from childhood, most people find they cannot climb free of religion later in life. Many find it impossible to shed this ingrained religious influence, even if they blossom into scientists or technologists. Education helps them carve out their careers, but they practice religion as they always have. Before you believe in anything, science demands that it be subjected to inquiry, analysis, and proof. If something cannot be proven, it should not be blindly believed. But around the world, the educated exempt religion from the scientific scrutiny they apply to everything else. When religion and science conflict, most people follow religion and give science a pass. Religion stands revealed as a barrier to human development. They do not apply the scientific temperament acquired in the course of their education to matters of religion.

Parents Fail to Stand Up to Religion

Beholden to their faiths or mired in tradition, parents have too often stood mute, helpless spectators to the religious abuse of children. Examples include denial of health care to children, practiced by several Christian denominations; widespread sexual abuse of children by Roman Catholic and other clergy; female genital mutilation as practiced under Islam and some traditional African religions; cruel corporal punishment under Sharia law; ostracism of low-caste children, child marriage, and temple prostitution under Hinduism; and male infant circumcision, originated by Judaism. If the civilized world is sometimes outraged by such abuses, it has nonetheless kept quiet, afraid to confront religion head-on. Individuals have dared to criticize religious child abuse, only to be ignored or ostracized as "atheists."

Fortunately, some light shimmers along this dark horizon.

UN agencies . . . will not identify religion among the principal causes of abuse.

Proclaiming Children's Rights

On November 20, 1989, the United Nations General Assembly adopted the Convention on the Rights of the Child, proclaiming elementary rights for children worldwide. One hundred ninety-one countries have so far adopted it. In many of them, so-called Children's Charters have been established, building key provisions of the UN Convention on the Rights of the Child into local law. Still, the so-called Children's Convention has not been ratified everywhere. Somalia, wracked by civil war and without a stable government, has not done so. Nor has the United States.

The Children's Convention covers all children below eighteen years of age, recognizing legal rights whose respect is incumbent upon parents, families, and governments. It forbids discrimination based on caste, color, creed, or gender in safeguarding children's rights. Under the Convention, every girl and boy, irrespective of territorial boundaries, enjoys freedom of expression and the right to access information. Governments are to safeguard children's religious freedom, their freedom of thinking, and their right to mix with others. Child rearing is recognized as the primary responsibility of parents, but governments must extend a helping hand when needed. Children are not to be treated as the personal property of parents, and they are not to be abused.

Obviously the Children's Convention describes the way things should be, not the way they are in most parts of the world. To its credit, the United Nations has recognized that the Convention's ideals are often violated. The United Nations Children's Fund (UNICEF) has launched a movement to safeguard children from abuse—but this movement is of limited effectiveness because it has tried to proceed without blaming religion. Religious influence is strong, even at the UN. For example, the Vatican has co-opted UNICEF, convening a recent conference at which religious leaders shed crocodile tears over children's plight but took no substantial action. Child abuse rooted in religion was described in sanitized language as a "cultural crisis."

UN agencies have recognized that children are being used as bonded labor, abused in wars, sexually assaulted, and more. They have striven to rescue victims in some places. But they will not identify religion among the principal causes of abuse. Child abuse is impossible to resist when the principal perpetrator cannot—must not—be named. We cannot expect religions to condemn themselves. It is like handing our house keys to a thief with a request to stand guard.

Children and Religion:
Some Immodest Proposals

Those who escaped from religion have contributed disproportionately to progress and development in all ages. The urge to learn new things, to study, to conduct research, and to live in tune with nature . . . all of these things belong to a level above religion. When children are inculcated in religion and compelled to adhere to it, this thwarts brain development. It is a crime to warn children that they will lose their sight or fall ill if they refuse to worship god or raise unpalatable questions—or it should be. Brains that should blossom with each passing year are instead blunted. And the priests have no objection because a thinking soul is a threat to every religion.

Religion should be taught on scientific lines in schools. Children should learn about all religions, their own and others. They should be taught that gods and demons, devils and apparitions, heaven and hell are all human creations, and that the world's scriptures are all human works. They should learn that life is supreme and it should be respected. Children should have the freedom to choose any religion or none once they reach the age of maturity.

For their part, parents should realize that religion ought not to be ascribed to children as a hereditary trait. Indeed, they should be kept at a distance from religion, just as parents keep them away from prostitution, politics, obscenity, and marriage. Taking children to temples, modifying their bodies (whether temporarily or permanently) in accord with ritual, encouraging blind worship, and terrorizing them in the name of a deity are no longer acceptable. Parents need to appreciate and accept that children have inherent rights.

One hundred ninety-one countries have signed the Children's Convention, and their parliaments have begun to adopt charters and other legislation to implement it. But it has yet to be adopted by a developed country like the United States because of religious opposition. Even parents hesitate to support the Convention, for fear of losing their grip on their children. Parents may have been brought up entangled in a religious tradition. But they should not impose their rituals, customs, habits, and superstitions on their children as a forced legacy. Now is the day to break with this unhealthy past.

Ultimately, human progress depends on the recognition that all religions are ultimately opposed to human values. The very assertion that we live for God is contrary to human values. Children should be rescued from religion; only then can they be restored to humanity.

Family Preservation Policies Exacerbate Child Abuse

Anna Gorman

Anna Gorman is a Los Angeles Times *staff writer.*

When paramedics arrived at Rocio Santoyo's El Sereno [California] home just after noon on Aug. 20, [2004], they found an ominous sign on the door: "Abandon All Hope Ye Who Enter Here."

Inside the one-story stucco house, they discovered Santoyo unconscious in a bathtub full of water, a wrist slit and her neck punctured. In a nearby bedroom, they found Santoyo's 10-year-old son blindfolded and bleeding to death from a deep gash in his neck. Scribbled on the wall above him were the words: "Walter, I told you. I hate you. Now U really only have 3 kids."

Santoyo lived. Her son, Salomon, did not. Now Santoyo, who had regained custody of the boy just four days before his death, is accused of his murder. She has pleaded not guilty.

Child Protective Agencies Make Fatal Errors

Salomon's death is [just one] in a succession of child murders . . . in which children who had been removed by the county from abusive or neglectful situations died after being returned to their parents' homes.

Salomon's case, documented in confidential court records, . . . starkly demonstrates how the child welfare system, designed to protect abused and neglected children, sometimes fails them miserably. "Life is just not a crystal ball," said Los Angeles County Superior Court Judge Michael Nash, who presides over the juvenile court. "The system has never worked as well as it should. But it is moving in the right direction." Nash said he could not discuss Santoyo's case, citing the criminal charges, but said that children's safety is always the top priority in placement decisions.

Salomon was returned home after 16 months in foster care under the guidelines of family reunification, a philosophy now part of California law that endeavors to return children to once-abusive homes after the parents have successfully completed such requirements as counseling and parenting classes, and are considered no longer likely to harm their children. The law, enacted in 1984, states that the goal of social service agencies and courts should be to "preserve and strengthen" the family wherever possible and that reunification should be a "primary objective."

It has resulted in tens of thousands of California families being safely and successfully reunited after receiving help from social workers and therapists. But it also has led to children's deaths because the policy relies on people trying to predict behavior as they balance keeping families together with keeping children safe.

The incident [of reported abuse] was considered 'unsubstantiated,' . . . and Salomon remained in his mother's care.

About 10,000 children in Los Angeles County are removed from their parents' custody each year because of abuse or neglect. Roughly 5,000 children are returned home annually. Of those reunited with their families, about 3%—or 170 children a year—are removed again, according to the county Department of Children and Family Services.

"There is always a risk involved," said Miriam A. Krinsky, executive director of the Children's Law Center of Los Angeles. "The real challenge for the courts, for social workers and for lawyers is to assess those risks and make those tough decisions. It's very difficult to fully know everything there is to know. That's why tragedies, unfortunately, do happen."

Abusive Parents Are Determined to Get Their Children Back

Salomon first came to the attention of county authorities in 1995, when social workers received a call alleging abuse and found a red mark on one of the boys legs. The incident was considered "unsubstantiated," according to court records, and Salomon remained in the mother's care.

Then, on April 23, 2003, the sweet-natured, dark-haired boy arrived at Farmdale Elementary School in tears. He told his teacher that his mother had hit him 13 times with a belt because he couldn't find his sneakers. Salomon, who had several bruises, said he was scared she wouldn't stop until he found them.

The school nurse called police, who arrested Santoyo. Salomon was placed in foster care. Social worker Ophelia Garnica concluded in an April 28 report that the boy would be "at continued risk of abuse" if returned to his mother.

After social workers placed Salomon in foster care, Santoyo seemed determined to get the boy back.

Santoyo admitted to social workers that she had "lost it" with her son and said she needed help. But she insisted that the abuse was out of the ordinary. "I know what I did was wrong, but this is an isolated incident," she said, according to court records. "I don't mistreat my son."

Salomon's statements suggested otherwise. The boy told authorities that his mother had hit him "too many times to count," according to court records. Asked by social worker Stacy Holland about his mother nearly two months after he entered foster care, Salomon said he still sometimes felt afraid of her.

"Do you miss your mother?" Holland asked.

"I'm missing her a little," he responded. "But if she never hit me, I'd say I'm missing her a lot."

After social workers placed Salomon in foster care, Santoyo seemed determined to get the boy back. Holland recommended that Santoyo take parenting classes, participate in individual therapy and attend joint counseling with her son, which she agreed to do.

At a juvenile court hearing soon after Santoyo lost custody, Commissioner Brian Petraborg granted her monitored visits with Salomon, ordering her not to hit the boy. On July 15, when Santoyo pleaded no contest to child abuse in criminal court, Judge Dennis Aichroth sentenced her to three years' probation, 45 days of Caltrans work and one year of parenting classes.

From the time of Salomon's placement in foster care, the goal of those charged with his oversight was reunification [with his family].

Santoyo was at the same time attempting a reconciliation of a different sort. Salomon's father, Walter Roa, had been estranged from Santoyo since his son's birth. But on hearing of Salomon's placement in foster care, Roa, a former gang member with a criminal conviction for selling drugs, began trying to rebuild a relationship with Santoyo and Salomon, and eventually left his wife and two children.

The court soon granted Roa permission to visit with his son but instructed him to participate in drug counseling and testing, along with parenting classes and therapy with his son.

From the time of Salomon's placement in foster care, the goal of those charged with his oversight was reunification. California's laws—and those of many other states—stem from research showing that, if they can be kept safe, children are better off with their parents because of strong biological and family ties.

The laws had the worthy goal of reducing the number of children languishing in foster care without any plans for returning them home or finding them permanent alternatives with relatives or adoptive parents. But they also have produced tragedies.

"If you can assist the family to come back together in a way that is safe, the children will ultimately benefit, as well as the parents," said Nancy Wright, a professor at Santa Clara University School of Law. "In this case, it sounds like a tragic error was made."

Agencies Do Not Accurately Assess the Risks

By Aug. 16 of [2004], Santoyo, 28, had completed her parenting classes and therapy. She had visited with her son regularly without any problems and had been allowed unsupervised, overnight visits with him at her home in northeast Los Angeles.

Social workers had repeatedly voiced concerns that Santoyo needed more therapy. But the county Department of Children and Family Services can recommend against reunification only if there is evidence that the child would be at risk if returned home, according to the county counsel's office. Deeming there was no evidence of such risk, the department recommended in an Aug. 16 report that "Salomon return home to his mother," with the help of its family preservation services.

Social workers tried to assess the situation as best they could, said department spokeswoman Louise Grasmehr, and Santoyo appeared to be doing well.

"But we're dealing with human beings, and we can't always predict what will happen," she said. "It's heartbreaking for everybody."

Everyone involved in the case agreed that Salomon should go home, said Kenneth Sherman, a lawyer whose firm represented the boy. Salomon was no longer scared of his mother, he said, and the system had moved "deliberately and slowly" in an attempt to ensure his safety.

Santoyo's therapist, Gloria Guevara, wrote a letter in July stating that Santoyo was working to improve her parenting skills, express her anger and resolve conflicts.

"Ms. Santoyo has expressed a strong desire to be reunified with her son," Guevara wrote. "It is this therapist's opinion that she has made enough improvement to be given an opportunity to be reunited with her son."

Another therapist who saw Santoyo and her son together twice, Wendy Thomas, wrote on Aug. 9 that they had made progress and their interactions were "appropriate." Thomas told the social worker that she did not have any concerns with reunification, according to court records.

Following the recommendations, Judge Jan Levine ruled that there was no longer a risk of harm to Salomon and that he could go home.

All Facts Are Not Known

But social workers and lawyers now say they didn't know all the facts when recommending that Salomon go home. They were unaware, for example, that seven months earlier, on Jan. 16, Santoyo had tried to kill herself with vodka and Vicodin. On that occasion, Santoyo was hospitalized after her roommate and longtime friend, Teresa Leyva, found her in the bathtub, according to a Los Angeles Police Department investigative report written after Salomon's death.

Santoyo said she was upset because she was unable to pay her bills, the report stated. At first, Santoyo was being held at the hospital, the report stated. A few days later, she checked herself out, despite a doctor's recommendation that she stay longer.

In addition, pressures were building for Santoyo in the weeks before Salomon went home. She was fired from her job at a collection agency for missing too much work, both for court appearances and because of persistent migraine headaches, Leyva said.

"Anything would set her off," Leyva said. "She had an anger problem."

Leyva said she knew something was wrong when she arrived home and saw blood on the bathroom floor.

The System Fails Children

There also was tension between Santoyo and Roa.

On Aug. 20, according to a police report, Santoyo confronted Roa, accusing him of not telling her that he had a fourth child. Police believe that may have been what sent her over the edge. She angrily threw his clothes in a box and broke the birthday gifts he had given her just days earlier, including a mirror decorated with dragons.

After Santoyo calmed down, Roa told Salomon that everything would be OK and headed to work. Later that morning, Leyva called him and said Santoyo was going "mad," the police report stated. Leyva promised him she would check on Salomon and Santoyo during her lunch hour.

Leyva said she knew something was wrong when she arrived home and saw blood on the bathroom door. She found Salomon covered in blood on his mother's bed, and Santoyo unconscious in the bathroom.

"Rocio, Rocio, what did you do?" Leyva screamed.

Paramedics discovered Santoyo in the tub with two knives; an empty bottle of migraine medicine was nearby. She had slit her wrist and punctured her own neck, according to the police report. Salomon died of his wounds 20 minutes later at a hospital.

"This is probably the worst of the cases I've handled," said LAPD Det. Tina Certeza. "None of us, not even the family, could understand it. . . . They didn't see this coming."

Santoyo is in county jail, with bail set at $1 million. If convicted, she could be sentenced to life in prison.

Defense attorney Leslie Stearns said she was looking into her client's mental health. "She's very sad for the loss of her child," she said, declining to comment further.

One of Salomon's foster parents, Gina Rodriguez, said she is angry that the system failed the boy.

"Something had to have fallen through the holes for him to be put back so soon with that kind of result," said Rodriguez, a minister who has been a foster parent for 11 years. "Something was missed. Something didn't get noticed. Something didn't get reported."

CHAPTER 3

How Can Society Reduce Child Abuse?

Chapter Preface

Countless remedies have been proposed to prevent child abuse. Some commentators argue that parents should be licensed so that their parenting abilities can be assessed before they actually have children. Another proposal mandates that parents addicted to drugs or alcohol should lose custody of their children. Those supporting this approach note that more child abuse occurs in homes where drug and alcohol use is high. Parenting classes, drug treatment, improved social services, and tougher laws are also presented as panaceas to this serious problem. However, all of these approaches have their critics, making it difficult to create a comprehensive plan to reduce the incidence of child abuse. One especially controversial proposal is chemical castration for sex offenders.

College biology student Katherine Amlin researched the advantages and disadvantages of chemical castration, in which males are given female hormones to inhibit the production of testosterone. Testosterone plays a key role in male aggression and sex drive. After completing her research, she concluded that "when used as a mandatory condition of parole, chemical castration decreases the occurrence of repeat offenses from 75 percent to 2 percent." This approach to preventing child abuse rests on two assumptions: that sex abusers cannot control their sexual impulses and that hormone injections can cure their violent behavior.

Many convicted abusers are signing up for castration in exchange for shorter prison terms. However, many experts worry that as soon as abusers are no longer required to take the chemicals—when their probation terms end—they are likely to offend again. Additionally, many critics contend, chemical castration instills a false sense of security in the community where the abuser resides. As Florida prosecutor Jerry Burford states, "I get a lot of people who are impotent that still commit sexual battery. It's not their gonads that cause them to commit sexual battery; it's their heads."

There are no simple solutions to the child abuse problem. Each proposal has its supporters and its critics. This chapter explores many of the most popular approaches to protecting children from abuse.

Fighting Poverty Would Reduce Child Abuse

Carlos I. Uresti

Carlos I. Uresti is a Democratic congressman from Texas.

Preventing child abuse and neglect requires both a willingness to address its underlying causes and an ability to break the chain of generational violence that is its hallmark.

Our child welfare system tries to break the generational chain of violence largely through the state's foster care system. However, often by the time a child is actually removed from an abusive environment, it is fair to point out that, sadly, the damage is done. . . . Child Protective Services and foster care reforms will go a long way toward improving outcomes for children already in abusive situations. Caseloads will fall, caseworker training will improve, and response times to reports of abuse will be shortened with a more efficient use of staff and technology.

Poverty and Dead Children

However, these reforms do not and cannot reach the core of our child abuse and neglect problem. [We] still [have] much work to do on the causes of this epidemic. . . .

There is a connection between dead children and underfunded schools. But there are even stronger connections to be drawn between dead children and poverty, poor health care, teenage and unwanted pregnancies, substance abuse and mental illness.

Addressing the underlying causes of child abuse and neglect is the only real hope we have of reducing the number of gruesome cases we read about almost daily. . . .

Carlos I. Uresti, "Attack Poverty to End the Cycle of Child Abuse," *San Antonio Express News*, June 26, 2005. Reproduced by permission.

We know, for example, that substance abuse is a significant and increasing contributor to child abuse and neglect.

Yet treatment options for substance abuse remain underfunded—especially for women with children. Substance abuse problems are more likely to meet with incarceration than treatment. But treatment requires funding, and it also requires the will to help those who have made poor decisions, provided they also want to change their lifestyles.

We know there is one single risk factor connected to most of the other risk factors for child abuse and neglect: poverty.

Connections Between Poor Health Care and Abuse

We know children in poor health are also at a much higher risk of abuse or neglect, especially those with serious or chronic health problems or [who were] premature deliveries. Quality prenatal and postnatal health care for these children can greatly reduce one of the biggest factors leading to neglect. . . .

[Providing such care] will surely lead to a reduction of child abuse and neglect cases—if the will exists to embrace the idea that every child deserves good health care before and after birth.

We know there is one single risk factor connected to most of the other risk factors for child abuse and neglect: poverty. Attacking poverty does not mean creating a "business-friendly" economy where companies pay the lowest wages possible and escape their fair share of taxes.

Economic Development Is Needed

Attacking poverty requires the will to improve economic conditions for the population as a whole, not just big business and the top 10 percent. It requires the will to ensure that the basic needs of all ... are met and that good work at a fair wage is available to anyone who wants it. It also requires letting go of the belief that the poor deserve their poverty....

The importance of schools in creating opportunities for children to escape or deal with the risk factors that lead to abuse and neglect [is undeniable]. But the real job ahead of us is much harder than simply fixing public schools.

The job ahead of us involves repairing and revitalizing communities with sensible economic development, effective and affordable health care and progressive solutions to problems such as substance abuse, mental illness and teenage pregnancy. The job ahead of us requires committing ourselves to a community of vision and opportunity for all.

The job does not begin in the legislature, but rather with the voters who select representatives who reflect their priorities.

Better Support for Child Welfare Workers Can Reduce Child Abuse

Jess McDonald and Mary Bissell

Jess McDonald is the former director of the Illinois Department of Children and Family Services. Mary Bissell, an attorney and child advocate, is a fellow at the New America Foundation.

Americans who care about children and families should first resolve to improve the imperiled state of the nation's child welfare workers.

Sensational cases of child abuse and neglect have kept the spotlight on the failures of state child welfare agencies and the thousands of workers responsible for protecting children. These caseworkers, often the first responders in a family violence situation, must determine whether abuse or neglect has occurred, assess its severity, and make sure the child is safe—often within minutes of meeting the family. Unlike police, firefighters and other rescue workers, however, the public demands a higher standard of performance: perfect decision-making. Workers must often choose between taking a child from his family or subjecting him to the risk of further harm. No matter what the outcome, they know that the child is likely to suffer.

Social Workers Are Overworked and Underpaid

In addition to serious emotional stress, caseworkers generally carry a caseload anywhere from two to three times the recommended levels. Most end up spending 50 to 80 percent of

Jess McDonald and Mary Bissell, "No Holiday From Child Neglect," *Seattle Post Intelligencer*, September 1, 2005, p. B7. Seattle Post-Intelligencer. All rights reserved. Reproduced by permission.

their time on paperwork—precious hours that would be better spent in direct contact with children and families. Although mission-driven workers don't go into social services for the money, the Bureau of Labor Statistics reports that child protection work remains one of the five worst-paying professional jobs in the country with an average starting salary of only $22,000. The work is also dangerous. Seventy percent of frontline caseworkers reported they had either been threatened with violence or been a crime victim.

The double whammy of high stress and low pay makes it exceedingly difficult for child welfare agencies to recruit and retain talented social workers with the experience needed to handle complex cases. Annual turnover rates for caseworkers can run as high as 50 percent, and most workers leave child protection work for good after two years. Not only is constant turnover costly for financially strapped child welfare agencies, it is traumatic for the children in the system who are forced to establish a trusting relationship with yet another social worker.

Proper Training Is Not Always Available

The lack of proper training is also a chronic problem. Currently, one-third of child welfare workers have a social work degree or sufficient pre-service training to help them sort through complicated issues of substance abuse, domestic violence, mental illness and poverty. And instead of incentives for good performance, workers are often rewarded with larger caseloads and increased supervisory responsibilities.

Even in this state of emergency, there is good news— concrete solutions to ensure that child welfare workers are armed with the tools they need to keep children safe. The federal government can start by developing minimum caseloads, training and other appropriate requirements and conditioning federal child welfare funding—more than $20 billion per year—on states' implementation of these standards. Federal child welfare financing must also be overhauled to give states more flexibility and increased funding to give caseworkers, supervisors and child welfare administrators the training they need to improve the lives of children and families.

If the U. S. public is truly serious about preventing abuse . . . child welfare caseworkers and administrators must be given the financial and moral support they need to succeed.

Accountability Standards Are Needed

In exchange for necessary increases in federal and state child welfare investments, state agencies must demonstrate significantly better outcomes for children and families. For example, accountability standards on workforce-related issues should play a significant role in Child and Family Service Reviews— comprehensive federal evaluations of state child welfare agencies, to assure adequate caseloads, training procedures and hiring and retention practices.

These changes cannot be accomplished unless the public's outrage over highly publicized cases of child abuse and neglect is matched by a strong, ongoing commitment to improve the child welfare system. Unfortunately, public and political appetite for reform often falters once the latest abuse or neglect case disappears from the headlines. Media attention may be sufficient to get caseworkers and agency administrators fired, but it doesn't sustain the long-term changes that are needed to prevent future tragedies.

In the end, wrote Marc Parent, a former social worker in New York City, "Children don't fall through the cracks. They slip through human hands." If the U.S. public is truly serious about preventing abuse and neglect and helping children lead better lives, child welfare caseworkers and administrators must be given the financial and moral support they need to succeed. And while professional challenges never excuse mistakes, they trumpet the need for exhaustive system reform, because for the nation's most vulnerable children, there is no holiday from abuse and neglect.

Tougher Adoption Laws Are Needed to Thwart Internet Baby Sales

Ian Lamming

Ian Lamming is a staff writer for the Northern Echo, *a British newspaper.*

Floating in cyberspace, somewhere between the shiny new cars and the limited edition hardback books, are countless children, displaced, homeless and some for sale.

Their little faces stare appealingly from colourful websites, like fluffy kittens and puppies in the pet shops before Christmas.

"This handsome boy is ready for his forever family," states one. "Love at first sight," it adds, rather inappropriately given the child is obviously cross-eyed. "This little guy loves to play . . . If you know anyone interested in this little man contact . . ." The little man is two, the little man has no name, the little man has only a number.

More disturbing still are the older children up for grabs. They have learning difficulties, behavioural problems, medical disorders, many the result of their up-bringing so far, one whose problems began in the womb, thanks to an alcoholic mother.

It's a simple process to begin. Just type in the web address. The surfer is then given the opportunity to choose the sex, age, race and colour, location, level of intelligence and emotional, medical and physical disability of the child they're after. Whatever the moral perspective, the dotcom sites make sad reading, a testament to a world where too many children are suffering. . . .

Ian Lamming, "Exposing the Dotcom Baby Trade," *Northern Echo*, January 18, 2001, p. 10. Copyright Newsquest (North East) Ltd., 2001. Reproduced by permission.

More than 1,700 children have been adopted from 63 countries in all [between 1994 and 2001]; almost half have come from China.

It is totally unacceptable . . . that children are sold to the highest bidder.

But it's the case of Alan and Judith Kilshaw, of Buckley, North Wales, who gazumped [swindled] another adoptive couple and fled America with twins Kimberley and Belinda, that has set the world reaching for its soapboxes, debating the rights and the wrongs of buying humans on the Net.

It's an issue that has political rivals Tony Blair and William Hague in rare agreement in the House of Commons, and legislation tightening controls over parents adopting abroad is being rushed through.

Felicity Collier, chief executive of the British Agencies for Adoption and Fostering (BAAF), says the practice demonstrates why private adoption is illegal in the UK. "We often hear criticisms by prospective adopters about the checks which are carried out before adoptive parents are considered suitable and comparisons are made far too often with the ease with which people can adopt in the US," she says.

Background checks overseas on adoptive parents are not rigorous enough, leaving the children vulnerable to possible abuse.

"But children have a right to live in secure and loving families. Adults do not have an automatic right to adopt. It is totally unacceptable to BAAF that children are sold to the highest bidder. It is vital that people who wish to adopt from overseas take proper advice before they enter such a minefield."

It's a view echoed in County Durham. Head of services for children and their families, Ken Black, says: "I think it is very worrying that human life can be traded on the Internet at all.

"You wonder what is going to happen to these children later. Will they go through life thinking they could be snatched back?"

Money aside, there are other problems associated with adopting abroad. It is easier than in this country, where the system has been attacked for being too tortuous, too stringent, too restrictive.

But experts here claim background checks overseas on adoptive parents are not rigorous enough, leaving the children vulnerable to possible abuse.

Foreign countries have also been too quick to have children adopted in cases of state emergency, such as war and disaster. Children have found themselves being sent to new homes abroad when their parents are perhaps still alive.

"With inter-country adoption there's the concern that you are taking them away from their cultural roots," says Mr Black. "Often in countries in turmoil insufficient work is done to see whether they are orphans or have just been separated from their parents. So this is something that needs to be regulated carefully."

Adopting foreign children and bringing them to Britain can leave youngsters struggling with their identities. During their early years they don't realize they are different from their parents. Then school years can be particularly cruel and difficult as they try to come to terms with their backgrounds.

"Seeing the Romanian children in their orphanages must have been very hard for couples who didn't have children," says Mr Black. "I've no objection to inter-country adoption as long as it is done properly and legally. But buying children is a different thing."

There's no doubt that some couples wanting to have children are driven by a desperate need, a force which won't wait for the lengthy legal processes in this country and ultimately sends some abroad.

"We do need to speed up the adoption process here and make it clearer and more transparent," says Mr Black.

"There are people who have waited a long time, there are children to be adopted and the process moves too slowly. But there are new Government guidelines on adoption which the professionals working in the field support. And the Prime Minister wants to focus on not being so rigid on age, or whether the parents smoke, for instance."

Things are changing, and more quickly than adoptive parents have experienced in the past. So whatever the moral arguments surrounding the Internet children, some good may yet come out of the system.

Teen Parenting Classes Could Reduce Child Abuse

Catherine Roberts, Clara Wolman, and Judy Harris-Lobby

Catherine Roberts, Clara Wolman, and Judy Harris-Lobby are faculty members in the Graduate Exceptional Education Program at Barry University in Miami Shores, Florida.

The rate of reported child abuse fatalities has risen annually, with an estimated 1,400 child fatalities from abuse occurring in 2002 alone; even so, recent studies estimate that 50–60 percent of deaths from child abuse are not recorded. Whiplash and other symptoms of shaken baby syndrome (SBS) were reported as the cause of death in 17 percent of fatal child abuse cases.

Statistics indicate that many victims of such abuse are children of teenage parents. Parenting classes could lessen the prevalence of the problem, but such classes are under-utilized in this era of high-stakes testing. In particular, school curricula in special education do not adequately prepare students with special needs, particularly those with the most violent behaviors, for their most demanding job—parenting. Profiles of typical abuse perpetrators match the characteristics of many students with emotional and behavioral disorders (EBD). . . .

Parenting Classes Can End the Cycle of Abuse

Teaching students parenting skills may be the most cost-effective way to reduce violent and abusive behaviors and prevent the transfer of violent behaviors from generation to generation. For less than $1,000, Project Baby Care, a parental training program developed and adapted for adolescents with EBD, proved successful in increasing their parental knowledge and skills and improving their attitudes toward caring for an infant. The curriculum used in this project included two main components: 1) a practical component of hands-on experiences involving the interaction of students with computerized doll-babies, and 2) a traditional component of reading, writing, and watching films.

For added realism, participants were required to care for the baby while completing their class work.

Thirty-seven adolescents with emotional and behavioral disorders participated in this project. These students had been assessed by a multidisciplinary committee as having emotional and behavioral problems that were severe enough to warrant placement in four self-contained classes in an urban educational center in southeast Florida. The participants included 24 males and 13 females, roughly evenly divided between Hispanic and black students (African Americans and Haitians). The ages of the students in each class ranged from 14 to 20 years. Fifty-four percent of the students (n = 20) were known to the courts, including 50 percent of all participating males (n = 12) and 62 percent of all participating females (n = 8). Seventy percent of all the participants (n = 26) had been victims of recorded child abuse and/or neglect. Of the total number of participants, 63 percent of the males (n = 15) and 85 percent of the females (n = 11) had suffered child abuse and/or neglect. Seven female students (54 percent) who attended this program were mothers or pregnant at the time of data collection; two of these students were already mothers for the second time, and a third student with one child was pregnant with her second. Only four of the 24 boys had admitted fathering babies. This population is consistent with the data indicating that early onset of psychiatric disorders is associated with subsequent teen pregnancy among both males and females at a 33 percent greater rate than for other teens. The curriculum included both practical and traditional reading and writing components.

1) Practical Component: The interactive program in this project used two computerized life-size doll-babies that realistically simulated infant behavior (purchased from Baby Think It Over, Inc.) The two doll-babies used in this project were a light-skinned African American boy baby, and a Hispanic girl baby. Each doll-baby has a realistic head that requires support. The lifelike baby has a 21-inch long vinyl body, weighs approximately 6–7 pounds, and is anatomically correct. Each doll needs to be cared for by the student in very realistic, concrete ways: through feeding, burping, cuddling, and diapering. Each doll-baby has an internal computer that is programmed to cry at random intervals and/or when the doll's head is not being properly supported. As positive feedback, the baby coos and burps when the student provides proper handling.

Features of the Class

On average, each session of actual class instruction with a doll-baby lasted over 60 minutes, four times per week. The lifelike baby was used in various hands-on activities (e.g., changing the diaper). For added realism, participants were required to care for the baby while completing their class work. The internal computer was programmed to affect the baby's behavior (e.g., simulating a calm baby or a fussy baby). This feature allowed the teachers and counselors to adjust and tailor stressors in the environment, and to observe the students' reactions and strategies used in response. Students who mishandled the doll-baby were readily identified by the doll's loud, continuous cry. The internal computers detected and signaled the doll to cry if students failed to support the doll's head, neglected the doll, and/or roughly handled the doll. The computers produced perceptually louder and longer crying if the baby was shaken. Students interacted with the doll-babies only in the controlled setting of the classroom, and only when under observation by a counselor and at least one teacher during each session. The limitation of having only one doll-baby per session for the 10 or 11 students in each class placed some time limitations on total parenting time with the doll-babies.

2) Reading and Writing (Traditional) Component: The curriculum was adapted from a project called the Nurturing Program for Teenage Parents and Their Families. This project also used a series of paperback books called *The Parent Guidebooks for Growing Families*. The latter were particularly useful in teaching students who were nonreaders or very low readers the appropriate expectations for the stages of infant development; the series has excellent graphics that facilitated reading. Films also are used.

The researchers adapted both components of the program to better serve the EBD population. The program was written on a 5th- and 6th-grade reading level, although the content interest was geared for adolescent/young adult interests. Modeled behaviors included: additional, repetitive activities, such as rocking the baby when it continued to cry; proper car-seat positioning; increased use of discussions and group counseling sessions (e.g., strategies to prevent frustration when the baby continued to cry); proactive methods of discipline (e.g., re-direction techniques, time-outs); creative role-playing (e.g., telling your parent you are going to be a parent, scenarios on being a single parent); and preparation of materials at a lower reading level, when needed.

Project Baby Care was included as part of the required Life Skills Management course. Each student received a grade for the 20-session course. Six current teachers at the center provided major support for this project. At the conclusion of the project, students in all four classes attended an awards ceremony and pizza party in recognition of their efforts to become better parents.

The researchers provided the curriculum to teachers in the program. Two overriding concepts were integral to all aspects of the curriculum: 1) discipline, don't hit the child, and 2) talk to and play with the child. One meeting was held with the teachers to review the program, stress the program's two main concepts, and discuss instructional strategies and their implementation. Training was not necessary, as the curriculum was self-explanatory and the teachers were already trained and competent in working with this special needs population. All program materials (e.g., films, lessons, books, pamphlets) were located in the office and available to the staff.

A few students refused to touch the doll-baby at all, and showed either total disregard or outright hatred for the baby, especially when it cried.

Counselors Assist Students

The efforts of three counselors associated with the program greatly enhanced its effectiveness. As part of their general duties, counselors were encouraged to observe the students in their assigned classes and initiate group activities. Their presence and the varied roles they played during the intervention increased its effectiveness. They were present in the classes during each scheduled lesson to encourage class discussions, field questions, observe inappropriate or abusive behaviors, and provide psychological support. Many of the topics led the students to recall past experiences that, in some instances, were upsetting; the counselors provided a comfort zone for the students. Requests for private counseling sessions were immediately honored.

During the sessions, counselors and staff noted certain anomalies. A few students refused to touch the doll-baby at all, and showed either total disregard or outright hatred for the baby, especially when it cried. All but one of these students were male. More important, two of these students resided in homes with younger siblings; one of these students resided with a sibling under 5 years old. A few other students appeared to abuse the doll-babies (i.e., tossing the baby, pulling the baby, twisting the skin of the baby, and shaking the baby) or tried to ignore it (refusing to hold the baby). In all but one instance, these abusive behaviors appeared when the students were unable to stop the doll-babies from crying. Only once did a male student initiate aggression against a quiet doll-baby. It is important to note that other students in the class immediately showed indignation and reported the incident to the counselor, teachers, and other students. On two occasions, this type of incident almost caused a fight as a student went to protect the doll-baby from another student's inappropriate behavior. Counselors added additional sessions of private counseling for those participants who exhibited abusive and/or neglectful behaviors. Also, they spoke with parents, guardians, and foster parents about participants' exhibited inappropriate behaviors. In two instances, a family social worker was assigned to the home. . . .

This program significantly reduced students' beliefs in the need for corporal punishment.

Evaluating the Program

Before and after the project (pre- and posttest), students were administered two questionnaires: The Adult Adolescent Parenting Inventory and Test Your Nurturing Knowledge. The results showed that this program was very effective in three years:

- Knowledge About Parenting and Parenting Skills. This construct on knowledge about parenting reflects an understanding of the different stages of growth and development of a child, and the skills needed in the care and nurturing of a child. Comparison of pre- and posttest scores showed a strong increase in knowledge about parenting and parenting skills. . . . Participants who were already parents were more knowledgeable than others before the project started but still gained additional knowledge from the curriculum intervention on parenting.

- Beliefs About [Not] Using Corporal Punishment With Children. The students' beliefs about [not] using corporal punishment with children showed the greatest positive change as a result of this project. . . . High post-intervention scores on this belief indicate that participants value alternatives to corporal punishment, refute the need for physical force, consider democratic rule-making that includes all family members, and respect children's needs as part of a mutual parent-child relationship. Success in reducing the belief of an at-risk EBD population in the necessity of using corporal punishment to discipline children was a primary goal of this study.

- Empathy for the Child's Needs. Empathy refers to the ability of a person to be concerned about the needs and feelings of another. Empathic parents are sensitive to the needs of their children and create nurturing environments conducive to the intellectual, emotional, and social growth of their children. The authors observed increases from pre- to posttest scores in the students' empathy. . . . This significant growth in awareness of children's needs indicated that the techniques used in the curriculum to increase empathic attitudes were effective.

This study demonstrated that students with EBD can be successfully trained in appropriate parenting skills. Sixty-eight percent of the surveyed students stated that the Project Baby Care program had helped them to recognize that "parenthood brought dramatic life changes" and were now aware of how unrealistic their expectations about their abilities to parent had been.

Most important, this program significantly reduced students' beliefs in the need for corporal punishment. During the program, they learned more effective and humane ways to discipline a child.

A parenting curriculum aimed at strengthening competencies and coping resources in an EBD population can provide a proactive approach to successful transition into adulthood and promote positive life skills.

Prospective Parents Should Be Licensed

Peg Tittle

Peg Tittle has taught applied ethics for several years and has worked with children and adolescents in various capacities. She is a columnist for Philosophers' Magazine *online philosophy café and the editor of* Should Parents Be Licensed? Debating the Issues.

We have successfully cloned a sheep. It is not unreasonable, then, to believe that we may soon be able to create human life. And I'm sure we'll develop carefully considered policies and procedures to regulate the activity, perhaps if only because we have Mary Shelley's *Frankenstein* lurking in our minds.

For example, I doubt we'll allow someone to create his own private work force or his own little army. And I suspect we'll prohibit cloning oneself for mere ego gratification.

I imagine we'll enforce some sort of quality control, such that cloned human beings shall not exist in pain or be severely substandard with respect to basic biological or electrochemical functioning.

And I suspect one will have to apply for a license and satisfy rigorous screening standards. I assume this will include not only meeting certain requirements with regard to the lab and its equipment, but also submitting, and obtaining approval of a detailed plan regarding the future of the cloned human being; surely we won't allow a scientist to create it and then just leave it in the lab's basement one night when he leaves.

The thing is, we can already create human life. Kids do it every day.

Peg Tittle, "We License Plumbers and Pilots—Why Not Parents?" *Seattle Post-Intelligencer*, October 3, 2004. © 1998–2005 Seattle Post-Intelligencer. Reproduced by permission.

Children Deserve a Licensed Parent

And although we've talked ourselves silly and tied ourselves in knots about ending life—active, passive, voluntary, coerced, premeditated, accidental, negligent—we have been horrendously silent, irresponsibly laissez-faire about beginning life. We would not accept such wanton creation of life if it happened in the lab. Why do we condone it when it happens in bedrooms and backseats?

It should be illegal to create life, to have kids, in order to have another pair of hands at work in the field or to have more of us than them. It should be illegal to create a John Doe Jr. to carry on the family name and/or business.

And it should be illegal to knowingly create a life that will be spent in pain and/or that will be severely substandard.

We already license ... plumbers ... and television repairmen.... Are our TV sets and toilets more important to us than our children?

As for the screening process, would-be teachers are generally required to study full-time for at least eight months before the state will allow them the responsibility of educating children for six hours a day once the kids become 6 years of age. Many would say we have set the bar too low.

And yet we haven't even set the bar as high—in fact we haven't set a bar at all—for parents. Someone can be responsible not only for a child's education but for virtually everything about the child, for 24 hours a day until that child is 6 years of age—that is, for the duration of its critical, formative years—and he or she doesn't even have to so much as read a pamphlet about child development.

As Roger McIntire notes, "We already license pilots, salesmen, scuba divers, plumbers, electricians, teachers, veterinarians, cab drivers, soil testers and television repairmen.... Are our TV sets and toilets more important than our children?"

Then again, wait a minute—we have set a bar for parents: adoptive/foster parents. Those would-be parents have to prove their competence. Why do we cling to the irrational belief that biological parents are automatically competent—in the face of overwhelming evidence to the contrary? We have, without justification, a double standard.

Good Parenting Is a Social Responsibility

One common response to this notion of licensing parents is dismissal with a giggle, as if I'm suggesting the presence of police in the bedroom. But there is no necessary connection between sex (whether or not it occurs in the bedroom) and reproduction (unless, of course, you reject all forms of contraception), so that response indicates an error of overgeneralization. On the other hand, sex can make you a parent only in the biological sense; since I'm proposing that we license both parentage (the biological part of being a parent—the provision of sperm, ovum, and/or uterus) and parenting (the social part of being a parent—the provision of care, very comprehensively defined), the response also indicates an error of undergeneralization.

One must . . . be careful about distinguishing between moral rights and legal rights.

Another response to licensing parents is a sort of goofy incomprehension, often followed with something like "Well, it's not as if people plan it, you know—usually, it just happens." Excuse me? It is not possible to create life "by accident"—men don't accidentally ejaculate into vaginas and women don't accidentally catch some ejaculate with their vaginas. (As for failed contraception, there's morning-after contraception and abortion.) "I created someone by accident" should be just as horrific, and just as morally reprehensible, as "I killed someone by accident." (At the very least, such "parents" should be charged with reckless or negligent reproduction.)

Yet another response is dismissal with indignation, because surely such a proposal violates our rights! But do we have the right to replicate ourselves, to create a person? And do we have a right to raise that, or any other, person? There are many good arguments claiming that we don't: for starters, merely having a capability doesn't entail the right to exercise that capability. (Ruth Chadwick has written a good article examining various motives for having kids—she finds them all inadequate as grounds for the right to have them.) There are also many good arguments for claiming that such "rights" are better conceived as responsibilities or even privileges.

Rights Come with Responsibilities

One must also be careful about distinguishing between moral rights and legal rights. (Laura Purdy has written an excellent article investigating whether it's immoral to have children when there's a good chance they'll have a serious disease or handicap and David Resnik has written about whether genetic enhancement is immoral or unjust—neither advocates parenting licenses, but their conclusions are nevertheless relevant; for example, if it is immoral to have children with genetic defects, that might serve as a premise supporting parent licensing.)

But even if we do have the right to be a parent or to parent, no right is absolute. My rights end where your freedoms begin. The real question is under what conditions do we have those rights and, then, under what conditions are those rights violated. Why, for example, should the right to be a parent depend on the means of becoming a parent? People seeking access to new reproductive technologies are screened for genetic anomalies, infectious diseases and other "high-risk factors"; they must read and understand information about the risks, responsibilities and implications of what they are undertaking; and they must undergo counseling that addresses their values and goals.

Why should children born as a result of assisted insemination or in vitro fertilization be privileged to a higher standard of care in their creation than children born as a result of coitus? These questions about rights are not easy questions to answer, and this particular dismissal of the proposal to license parents reveals gross naiveté.

We could administer the [contraceptive] vaccine as a matter of routine, perhaps once puberty is reached.

A Simplified Licensing Procedure

Yet another dismissal appeals to the difficulty or impossibility of implementing the idea: Who would set the requirements, what would those requirements be, how would they be assessed . . . ? Often lurking beneath these concerns is one more: "and I suppose I wouldn't be good enough!" Partly, this is a paper tiger response: The more ridiculous the claim, the easier it is to mock, so people imagine all sorts of complicated and unrealistic policies and procedures that no advocate of parent licenses would ever suggest. . . .

And partly, paradoxically, this response reveals a failure of the imagination: Licensing parents could be as simple as when you turn 18, you get the book and study it or take the course, then you take the written test, and the eye test, and if you pass, you get a beginner's license, then you do some hands-on child care for maybe six months under the guidance of a licensed parent, and if you pass that part, you get your license, and if you don't, maybe you try again in a while. Sound familiar? So what's the problem?

Well, those bedrooms and backseats—we could never really control the parentage part. No, not at the moment. But what if we developed a contraceptive vaccination? (But nooo, our little boy scientists, once they'd finished snickering over the name "Dolly," developed Viagra instead.) We could administer the vaccine as a matter of routine, perhaps once puberty is reached. And then, as part of the license, the antidote could be made available.

Potential for Abuse vs. Benefits

One last objection concerns the potential for abuse. Do we really want to give the state this particular power? I have to say, seeing a theocracy coming ever closer, that this is the argument that gives me most pause.

Every year, millions of the people we've created so carelessly are being starved, beaten or otherwise traumatized.

I want to point out that just because something will be abused doesn't mean it shouldn't be tried, and I want to point out that our many other licensing policies still exist despite the occasional abuse. But I've read Margaret Atwood's "Handmaid's Tale." It's chilling. But I've also read the reports of people too drugged out to even know they're pregnant. And it's not a question of which scenario is more likely. One is already happening and has been for quite some time.

Most of us have seen broken kids, kids who didn't get what they needed at a critical stage in their development, so they go through life thinking the world owes them something. And indeed we do. But sadly, tragically, we can't give it to them because that critical window of time has passed: We can't go back and flush from the fetus the chemicals that interfered with its development; we can't go back and provide the baby with the nutrients required for growth; we can't go back and give the child the safety and attention that would have led to a secure personality. Every year, millions of the people we've created so carelessly are being starved, beaten or otherwise traumatized. Thousands die. And that doesn't count the ones still walking around.

To be succinct, the destruction of life is subject to moral and legal examination—so too should be the creation of life, whenever and however it occurs.

Funding for Child Abuse Prevention Programs Must Be Increased

Ross E. Cheit and Jennifer Freyd

Ross E. Cheit is associate professor of political science and public policy at Brown University, where he directs the law and public policy program at the A. Alfred Taubman Center for Public Policy and American Institutions. Jennifer Freyd is a University of Oregon professor of psychology and a fellow of the American Association for the Advancement of Science.

A tipping point has occurred in the debate about child sexual abuse, and we don't want you to miss it. For the first time, the influential journal *Science* has published policy recommendations aimed at helping our nation squarely face this uncomfortable problem in the context of the body of research to date. The article "The Science of Child Sexual Abuse," calls for the creation of a new Institute of Child Abuse and Interpersonal Violence within the National Institutes of Health [NIH].

Commonplace Realities

Research reveals that about 20 percent of women and five to 10 percent of men worldwide were victims of this crime as children. The pervasive climate of fear, social taboo and myth silences victims so effectively, however, that close to 90 percent of incidents don't get reported.

We all know about extreme cases—but can we face up to the more commonplace realities of child abuse? We hear every detail about Michael Jackson, a 46-year-old man who argues

Ross E. Cheit and Jennifer Freyd, "Let's Have an Honest Fight Against Child Abuse," *The Brown University Child and Adolescent Behavior Letter*, vol. 21, June 2005, p. 8. Copyright of Brown University Child & Adolescent Behavior Letter. Reproduced by permission of the authors.

that it's perfectly innocent to sleep with boys. We despair over recent murders in Florida at the hands of known sex offenders. But these cases—both examples of distracting extremes—tell us very little about the vast majority of child sexual abuse cases.

Most child sexual abuse is committed by a relative or someone known to the child, not by strangers or celebrities. This fact is so threatening to our social fabric that we hide from it. Such is the face of denial in the 21st century.

Known sex offenders represent a small fraction of predators, yet they receive the lion's share of the publicity. After all, even the Catholic Church acted only when "smoking gun" memos proved there was a cover-up—and not until 10 years after Cardinal [Bernard] Law blamed the *Boston Globe* for pursuing the story. Fortunately, such massive cover-ups are rare. Still, those who report sexual abuse face harsh scrutiny: a daunting prospect preventing many from coming forward.

Offenders Transform Themselves into Victims

Little thought is devoted to those who remain silent. The best evidence indicates that sexually abused children often keep it to themselves. At least for a while. When they do tell, the response—disbelief, denial, minimization and in some cases, even punishment—adds further devastation on top of the abuse.

Whereas $2 is spent on research for every $100 in costs for cancer, only $0.05 is spent for every $100 in costs for child maltreatment.

We call this DARVO, which stands for a three-step process: deny the behavior; attack the accuser; and reverse the roles of victim and offender. This strategy allows a truly guilty perpetrator to morph into "a victim of false accusations." The handful of highly publicized cases in which defendants were wrongly accused fuels a potent and destructive myth that any similar allegations also must be false.

Two common forms of denial are "It didn't happen" (or the similar "It rarely happens") and "It wasn't harmful." Put together these can take the form: "It didn't happen, but if it did, it wasn't that bad" or "It rarely happens, but when it does it isn't harmful." Such claims should raise red flags when made in defense of child sexual abuse allegations.

Sex between adults and children causes harm, no matter what you may hear elsewhere. The Department of Justice estimates rape and sexual abuse of children costs $24.5 billion per year. These crimes increase the risk of physical and mental illnesses, suicide, substance abuse and criminality. While many victims eventually recover, avoiding the worst of these problems, entrenched societal denial thwarts the healing process and leaves other children vulnerable to predators.

Society Fails to Act

We abhor child sexual abuse in the abstract, but as a society we fail to act against it. We have the science necessary to address this problem—we need the national will to do so.

We must employ every tool available to uncover the true extent of child sexual abuse so that destructive myths will forever be put to rest. Current efforts are embarrassingly meager. Whereas $2 is spent on research for every $100 in costs for cancer, only $0.05 is spent for every $100 in costs for child maltreatment.

Practical Solutions

There are practical avenues for addressing this shortfall. The National Child Traumatic Stress Network is a federally-funded network of 54 sites providing community-based treatment to children and their families exposed to a wide variety of trauma. We propose expanding that program by adding additional community-based treatment centers and increasing the support for associated research.

Finally, we propose the creation of a new Institute of Child Abuse and Interpersonal Violence within NIH to focus and coordinate research on causes, consequences, treatment, and prevention. This would also allow our country to open a visible and constructive chapter in the national discussion—one that will find better ways to prevent child abuse from occurring, while improving treatment for both perpetrators and their victims.

Individuals Can Help Reduce Child Abuse and Neglect

National Clearinghouse on Child Abuse and Neglect Information

The National Clearinghouse on Child Abuse and Neglect Information *was established in 1974 by the Child Abuse Prevention and Treatment Act to collect, organize, and disseminate information on all aspects of child maltreatment.*

As an individual and as a member of your community, you have the power to prevent child abuse and neglect. Here are some ways to contribute your ounce—or more—of effort to prevention.

Understanding, Support, and Activism

- *Understand the problem.* Child abuse and neglect affect children of all ages, races, and incomes. According to the National Child Abuse and Neglect Data System (NCANDS), in 2003, an estimated 906,000 children nationwide were victims of maltreatment. Most experts believe that actual incidents of abuse and neglect are more numerous than statistics indicate.

- *Understand the terms.* Child abuse and neglect take more than one form. Federal and State laws address four main types of child maltreatment: physical abuse, physical or emotional neglect, sexual abuse, and emotional abuse. Often more than one type of abuse or neglect occurs within families. Some types of maltreatment, such as emotional abuse, are much harder to substantiate than others, such as physical abuse.

National Clearinghouse on Child Abuse and Neglect Information, "You Have the Power to Prevent Child Abuse and Neglect," 2005. http://nccanch.acf.hhs.gov, 2005. Reproduced by permission.

- *Understand the causes.* Most parents don't hurt or neglect their children intentionally. Many were themselves abused or neglected. Very young or inexperienced parents might not know how to take care of their babies or what they can reasonably expect from children at different stages of development. Circumstances that place families under extraordinary stress—for instance, poverty, divorce, sickness, disability—sometimes take their toll in child maltreatment. Parents who abuse alcohol or other drugs are more likely to abuse or neglect their children.

- *Support programs that support families.* Parent education, community centers, respite care services, and substance abuse treatment programs help to protect children by addressing circumstances that place families at risk for child abuse and neglect. Donate your time or money, if you can.

- *Report suspected abuse and neglect.* Some States require everyone to report suspected abuse or neglect; others specify members of certain professions, such as educators and doctors. But whether or not you are mandated by law to report child abuse and neglect, doing so may save a child—and a family. If you suspect a child is being abused or neglected, call the police or your local child welfare agency.

- *Spread the word.* Help educate others in your community about child abuse and neglect. . . . Ask if you can leave a stack of brochures [on child abuse] at your local public library, recreation or community center, government center, or other public place. You also might make material available at your church, synagogue, mosque, temple, or other faith institutions. Even grocery stores usually have places to distribute community materials.

- *Strengthen the fabric of your community.* Know your neighbors' names and the names of their children, and make sure they know yours. Give stressed parents a break by offering to watch their children. Volunteer. If you like interacting with children, great, but you do not have to volunteer directly with kids to contribute to prevention. All activities that strengthen communities, such as service to civic clubs and participation on boards and committees, ultimately contribute to the well-being of children.

- *Be ready in an emergency.* We've all witnessed the screaming-child-in-the-supermarket scenario. If we are parents, at least once that screaming child has been ours. Most parents take the typical tantrum in stride. But what if you witness a scene—in the supermarket or anywhere else—where you believe a child is being, or is about to be, physically or verbally abused? Responding in these circumstances technically moves beyond prevention to intervention, and intervention is best handled by professionals. Still, if you find yourself in a situation where you believe a child is being or will be abused at that moment, there are steps you can take. Prevent Child Abuse America suggests the following:

- Talk to the adult to get their attention away from the child. Be friendly.

- Say something like, "Children can really wear you out, can't they?" or "My child has done the same thing."

- Ask if you can help in any way—could you carry some packages? Play with an older child so the baby can be fed or changed? Call someone on your cell phone?

- If you see a child alone in a public place—for example, unattended in a grocery cart—stay with the child until the parent returns.

Finally—and most important if you are a parent—remember that prevention, like most positive things, begins at home. Take time to re-evaluate your parenting skills. Be honest with yourself—are you yelling at your children a lot or hitting them? Do you enjoy being a parent at least most of the time? If you could benefit from some help with parenting, seek it—getting help when you need it is an essential part of being a good parent. Talk to a professional that you trust; take a parenting class; read a book about child development. Contact the resources to locate places that parents can get help.

CHAPTER 4

Will Changes in the Criminal Justice System Help Prevent Child Abuse?

Chapter Preface

Robert C., who does not wish his full name to be used, met with his scout troop each Wednesday to swim at a local pool. These outings turned horrific when his scout leader began sexually assaulting him in the pool and in the locker room. Robert buried his painful memories until he was in his thirties. By that time, however, the statute of limitations had run out for filing any criminal or civil charges against his abuser. Robert and other adult victims are now urging lawmakers to revise the laws, arguing that it can take decades before victims can confront their abusers. Currently, many states set limits of just a few years for filing charges against abusers.

Victims are now banding together to change laws in the hope that victims will be able to hold abusers accountable for their actions. Several states are now considering civil "windows" to expose predators and enablers, including anyone who ignored a sex crime, shielded a molester, destroyed documents relating to molestation, or deceived a victim's family. While those exposed would not be subject to criminal prosecution, supporters say that exposure would raise more awareness about abuse. Despite the growing popularity of civil windows, many activists are still working to change criminal laws relating to abuse, claiming that abusers must be punished, not just exposed.

One organization that advocates these changes in the law is the Survivors Network of Those Abused by Priests. It aims to pursue "justice and institutional change by holding individual perpetrators responsible and the church accountable." The fight to change abuse laws has intensified since the Catholic Church child sexual abuse scandal erupted in 2002. Numerous victims in the United States accused priests of abuse and church leaders of covering up the abuse. By the time these accusations were made, the statute of limitations against the church had run out, but it nonetheless agreed to settle claims with many of the victims. Attorney Carmen Durso, who represented many of these victims, believes that the church settled because of "the enormous publicity of the scandal." Durso believes that if the case were not a high-profile one, it would be highly unlikely that the abuser would settle. Thus, Durso and others contend, it is important to change statutes of limitation to enable victims to gain restitution long after the abuse occurred.

The public continues to be outraged by reports of abuse and the laws that allow predators to walk away without suffering consequences. The authors in this chapter debate the need for new, tougher laws that would help protect children from these abusers.

Tougher Laws Will Help Prevent Child Abuse

George W. Bush

George W. Bush is the forty-third president of the United States.

The PROTECT Act of 2003 will greatly assist law enforcement in tracking criminals who would harm our children and will greatly help in rescuing the youngest victims of crime. With my signature, this new law will formally establish the Federal Government's role in the Amber Alert system and will make punishment for Federal crimes against children more severe.

This law carries forward a fundamental responsibility of public officials at every level of government to do everything we can to protect the most vulnerable citizens from dangerous offenders who prey on them. . . .

Victims' Families Helped Create New Law

With us today are some families who understand better than most the need for this law. In your great suffering and loss, you have found the courage to come to the defense of all children. Because of you, this critical measure is now becoming law. Because of you, children and parents you may never meet will be spared from the harm and anguish your families have known. We are honored to have you all here today.

When a child is reported missing, that case becomes the matter of the most intensive and focused efforts by law enforcement. Entire communities join in the search, and through unrelenting efforts, many children have been saved.

Amber Alerts have become an increasingly important tool in rescuing kidnapped children, by quickly getting key infor-

President George W. Bush, "Remarks on Signing the Prosecutorial Remedies and Other Tools to End the Exploitation of Children Today Act of 2003." Weekly Compilation of Presidential Documents, May 5, 2003.

mation about the missing child and information about the suspect out into the public through radio broadcasts or highway signs or other means. An Amber Alert adds thousands of citizens to the search in the crucial early hours.

Amber Alert System Expanded

At present, statewide Amber Alert systems exist in 41 States. The bill I will sign this afternoon [April 30, 2003] authorizes matching grants to those and other States to help ensure that we have effective Amber Alerts wherever they are needed.

[In 2002], at my direction, Attorney General John Aschcroft appointed an Amber Alert coordinator to oversee this nationwide effort. This new law formally established that position and empowers the coordinator to set clear and uniform voluntary standards for the use of Amber Alerts across our country.

The new law ... confronts an evil that is too often a cause of child abuse, ... the evil of child pornography.

It is important to expand the Amber Alert systems so police and sheriffs' departments gain thousands or even millions of allies in the search for missing children. Every person who would think of abducting a child can know that a wide net will be cast. They may be found by a police cruiser or by the car right next to them on a highway. These criminals can know that any driver they pass could be the one that spots them and brings them to justice.

This is exactly what happened [in the summer of 2002] in California when several drivers heard an Amber Alert over the radio and soon passed a vehicle meeting the description they heard. Within hours, two teenage girls were rescued and their abductor cornered by the police. We're so happy these two young ladies are healthy and with us today, Tamara Brooks and Jacqueline Marris. . . .

The new law also confronts an evil that is too often a cause of child abuse and abduction in America, the evil of child pornography. In the past, prosecutors have been hindered by not having all the tools needed to prosecute criminals who create child pornography. Under the PROTECT Act, obscene images of children, even those created with computer technology, will now be illegal, giving prosecutors an important new tool. Obscene images of children, no matter how they are made, incite abuse, raise the dangers to children and will not be tolerated in America.

Stiffer Penalties

The new law will also strengthen Federal penalties for child kidnapping and other crimes against the young. Judges will now have the authority to require longer supervision of sex offenders who are released from prison. And certain repeat sex offenders in our society will now face life behind bars, so they can never do harm again.

In addition, this law creates important pilot programs to help nonprofit organizations which deal with children to obtain quick and complete criminal background information on volunteers. Mentoring programs are essential for our country, and we must make sure they are safe for the children they serve.

Amber Hagerman, whose mom is with us today, . . . was 9 years old when she was taken away from her parents. We are acting today in her memory and in the memory of so many other girls and boys who lost their lives in violence and acts of cruelty.

No child should ever have to experience the terror of abduction, or worse. No family should ever have to endure the nightmare of losing a child. Our Nation grieves with every family that has suffered unbearable loss. And our Nation will fight threats against our children.

This law marks important progress in the protection of America's children.

Giving Lie Detector Tests to Pedophiles Can Help Prevent Child Abuse

Barry Nelson

Barry Nelson is a staff writer for the Northern Echo, *a British newspaper.*

Keeping tabs on known paedophiles is one of the most difficult issues for the authorities. While sex offenders' details are known to the police and probation service and regular checks are made, there is no way of detecting what might be going on inside their heads after they have been released into the community.

Lie Detector Tests and a Pedophile's Intent

An early warning system that would alert the authorities to a paedophile who is about to start re-offending would be the answer to the prayers of probation workers and the police. Now Professor Don Grubin of Newcastle University, an expert on sex crime, has revealed that he is working on just such a system—and he believes it has already proved its worth.

Prof. Grubin, an American who has lived in the UK [United Kingdom] for 25 years, is sure that regular lie detector tests using an electronic polygraph, which are in widespread use in the United States, could help to alert the authorities when a paedophile is poised to strike again.

A scheme which used lie detectors to monitor sex offenders in the Southern state of Arkansas successfully cut re-offending rates, he says.

In the past the tabloids have run controversial campaigns to "out" paedophiles in the name of protecting children who may live on the same housing estate as an offender. This led to marches in towns like Portsmouth, in Hampshire, and attacks on completely innocent people suspected of being sex offenders.

A third of the sex offenders given polygraph tests by two American specialists had had unsupervised contact with children.

But most people would probably agree that there is still a very persuasive argument for keeping such details secret—the prospect of an offender going underground and being out of contact with police and probation officers.

So the idea of making paedophiles take regular lie detector tests as a form of early warning system has now surfaced as a serious proposal to control sex offenders in the community.

Test Results Are Encouraging

The polygraph trial, which involved tests on sex offenders in Northumberland, Surrey and the West Midlands [in 2001], was supervised by Prof. Grubin on behalf of the National Probation Service. They found that a third of the sex offenders given polygraph tests by two American specialists had had unsupervised contact with children.

Prof. Grubin, who is based at Newcastle University's Sexual Behaviour Unit, says three of the 30 men tested needed "significant action" to prevent them [from] re-offending.

Prof. Grubin is so encouraged by the results of the tests—which may have prevented paedophile attacks on unsuspecting North-East children—that he is in talks with the Home Office [Britain's department of domestic affairs] about running a much larger trial, this time involving up to 200 offenders. This would involve setting up a two-year scheme in three probation areas and comparing the findings with three areas where polygraphs are not used.

The tests take between 30 minutes and an hour with carefully structured questioning before, during, and after the polygraph is used. "The real skill is in the interviewing," say Prof. Grubin.

Other Methods Are Also Encouraging

This is not the first time that the Newcastle-based expert has been in the news because of his innovative work. Earlier . . . it was revealed that Prof. Grubin has been given permission by the Home Office to carry out tests to see whether the tranquilizing "happy pill" Prozac could be used to reduce the abnormal sex drives of convicted offenders. . . .

Prof. Grubin is convinced the drug will prove effective. "It is widely and successfully used for this purpose in the U.S., and I have used it to good effect in my own practice. It seems to work particularly well with men who repeatedly expose themselves," he says.

Tests Allow for Preventive Interventions

During [the 2001] lie detector trial the offenders were each asked questions about their past offending, current behaviour and fantasies.

Crucially, they were asked if they had been in contact with children or whether they were looking for new victims.

While there is skepticism about the reliability of polygraph tests . . . , Prof. Grubin is convinced they can play a useful role.

"Everyone disclosed information relevant to their rehabilitation," says Prof. Grubin. "About a third revealed unsupervised contact with children, and with three of them, we believe, if intervention had not been taken, they would have reoffended. The men themselves said as much afterwards."

The men told polygraph operators that they had deliberately gone to areas where they might meet children. "They were beginning to go in search of victims. They hadn't offended yet, but had no doubt in three of these cases [that] they would have done [so]," says the professor.

In one of the three cases where the test led to immediate action the subject was put back in a hostel, child protection proceedings were started against another and the third had his supervision increased.

It seems reasonable to use polygraphs if they are proved reliable.

Reliability Doubts

While there is scepticism about the reliability of polygraph tests in the UK, Prof. Grubin is convinced they can play a useful role. He says experience in America suggests that it is far harder to cheat lie detectors than many people thought. "Of course, anyone can beat the polygraph on an occasion, but around 90 per cent of the time people can't and that is the sort of level we need."

Most people's ideas of lie detectors come from American detective movies where the police are using it in an investigation, says the professor. "We are not talking about that at all, we are not talking about using it in court," he adds.

Eithne Wallis, a spokeswoman for the National Probation Service says the polygraphs could play a future role in monitoring sex offenders, if further tests prove that they are reliable. The Home Office is waiting for the results of the polygraph trial.

Polygraph examiner Sandy Gray, who comes from Arizona, says paedophiles are usually very skilled at being manipulative but says polygraph tests are "far better than simply accepting and taking their word for what they are doing".

Reliability Can Be a Key Factor

But Roger Stoodley, the senior detective who led the investigation into the paedophile network which included the notorious child killer Sidney Cooke, remains sceptical about the value of lie detectors. He says sex offenders are practiced liars and would be able to fool the most sophisticated equipment.

Paul Cavadino, chief executive of the National Association for the Care and Resettlement of Offenders (NACRO), says the issue of reliability is the key one. "If it is shown there is a high level of reliability, it would be perfectly reasonable to use polygraphs as part of the supervision and monitoring of sex offenders," he says.

Roger Bingham, a spokesman for the civil rights group Liberty, agrees: "It seems reasonable to use polygraphs if they are proved reliable, but they should not become a substitute for other safeguards used to monitor such offenders." But . . . as people cast their minds back to cases where men who have been recognized as a known danger to children were left to roam free in communities, and as residents of a housing estate in Dorset which has 17 sex offenders in the area yesterday angrily petitioned for their names to be made public, any early warning system which could stop paedophiles in their evil tracks merits serious consideration.

Unified Family Courts Would Help Prevent Child Abuse

Melinda Melendez

Melinda Melendez is a writer who has worked in politics and as an education adviser.

For some Florida families, a unified court can mean the difference between life and death.

According to the latest annual report of the *Florida Child Abuse Death Review*, of the 161 child deaths reviewed [since 2000], 92 children, or 57 percent, had five or more risk factors present at the time of the child's death. If you ask Barry Krischer, state attorney for the 15th Circuit, some of these deaths may have been prevented through the utilization of a unified family court.

The Legal System Contributes to Children's Deaths

"What all the numbers really mean is that we, and that includes the criminal justice system, family court, our juvenile court, DCF [Department of Children and Families], among others, knew of these children, and despite as many as five risk factors, we failed these children and we allowed them to die," said Krischer, who spoke at the Criminal Law Section luncheon at the Bar [Association]'s Annual Meeting. "That is unacceptable. We've failed because our approach has been disjointed and fragmented. And that occurs because we don't share information."

The unified family court is an integrated approach to handling all cases involving families and children. In many cases a family with multiple problems is forced into a variety of

Melinda Melendez, "It's Imperative for Family Courts to Communicate," *Florida Bar News*, vol. 32, August 15, 2005, p. 6. Copyright 2005 Florida Bar. Reproduced by permission.

courts. Under a unified family court structure, that family would have one judge preside over multiple issues affecting the family, instead of having to deal with issues singularly in family court, juvenile court, and criminal court.

"The 'one family, one court' concept recognizes that there are a number of different ways into the court system that different members of the same family can utilize for different reasons, at different times. The end result is a disorganized system, one that fails to meet the need for a holistic approach, one that results in an inconsistent and often times contradictory order," said Krischer.

We need resources to change these kids' behavior before they become the predators we so fear.

Krischer is certainly not alone in recognizing the need for a more cohesive family court structure, and the concept of a unified family court is not new. In 1991 the legislature's Commission of Family Courts issued a report to develop guidelines for the establishment of a family law division within each circuit, and gave recommendations for organizational changes and for necessary support services. The Florida Supreme Court issued three opinions between 1991 and 2001 that stated the need for a family court system to provide better protection for children in court and resolution of family problems. In May 2001, a fourth and unanimous opinion was issued that cited 12 principles as a guide to implementing a model family court, including that cases with interrelated family issues should be consolidated or coordinated.

For about four years, Pinellas County [Florida] has operated a unified family court using aid from a federal grant that allowed it to utilize the necessary technology for identifying families. Pinellas serves as the model for other counties, including Palm Beach County (which comprises the 15th Circuit), which will begin to explore technology options [in 2005].

Krischer is a strong advocate for adopting the unified court model. "Every aspect of that family and that child would go through one court. We have available to us the means and opportunity to save these children's lives. Prosecutors, defense counsel, and family court attorneys need to identify these families and work together to preserve the future of the children living in these homes that are exposed to violence. We must work together with the courts, not against each other to decrease domestic violence and family dysfunction. We cannot hope to make our streets safer if we don't make the effort to make our homes and children safe," said Krischer.

Proper Interventions Are Needed

One of the major incentives to adopt a unified family court, according to Krischer, is because children who end up in juvenile court are often exposed to violence in the home, thus creating an overlap of issues for a single family in juvenile and criminal court. "The question we should be asking is, 'How do we save these kids from a life of crime?' If we solve that problem, we might find that the notion of treating children differently from adults, simply because they are children, is not so ridiculous. These children, growing up in violent homes, that we fail to recognize as victims today, become tomorrow's abusers, the violent juveniles we prosecute in adult court," said Krischer.

Krischer, who has become somewhat notorious for bringing juveniles into adult court, suggests exploring the root of the problem instead of later dealing with the consequences. "The truth of the matter is [that] the reason I rely so heavily on adult sanctions in adult court is because of the juvenile court's shocking inability to impose meaningful penalties, and meaningful supervision. The one place I can deliver is in adult court. Why does it get that far? We need resources to change these kids' behavior before they become the predators we so fear.

"For every Nate Brazill, who shot and killed his teacher in front of a classroom full of students, who get all the attention, there are hundreds of other children around the state going through the juvenile court system. It's the Brazills that get the legislature's attention. But they respond by making the 10-20-life gun law apply to 15-year-olds. We can keep tinkering with the law; we can keep shipping children to adult court, but that does nothing to rescue the at-risk population before they become hardened criminals," said Krischer.

Unified Courts Could Address All Domestic Problems

Another difficulty faced by courts and agencies in dealing with families is the often specialized services offered by child welfare and domestic violence programs. Often the programs have the facilities to deal with one form of family violence, but according to Krischer, few programs effectively address whole forms of violence when they occur together in the same family.

"Courts regularly struggle with these issues individually, and out of the family context. Youth violence programs often fail to address the way that domestic violence impedes healthy development. That is yet another reason why model family court can incorporate innovative community collaborations between domestic violence agencies, child welfare agencies both public and private, the courts, school system, child protection teams, as well as health care providers, youth development organizations, and local churches. Each is integral in the resolution of cases in the model family court. Instead of five or seven courts making the same findings of fact and wasting limited judicial and community resources and trying to formulate a unique response to each family member, the model court treats the family as an organic whole," said Krischer.

Krischer closed his speech by underscoring the importance of moving to a unified court system as a matter of life and death for some kids and families.

"We can wait for the next child to witness domestic violence or the next drive-by-shooting, and lock up those kids after the damage is done, or we can rescue them one child at a time through the effort of establishing a unified court," said Krischer.

Laws Creating Pedophile-Free Zones Would Help Prevent Child Abuse

Traditional Values Coalition Education and Legal Institute

The Traditional Values Coalition (TVC) is the largest nonde-nominational, grassroots church lobby in America. Founded in 1980, with an emphasis on the restoration of the values needed to maintain strong, unified families, TVC focuses on issues such as education, homosexuality advocacy, family tax relief, pornography, the right to life, and religious freedom.

National attention is focusing on child sex offenders after the high profile case of repeat sex predator Joseph Duncan whose latest victim is a nine-year-old boy named Dylan Groene.

Duncan was first convicted in 1980 of sexually assaulting a 14-year-old boy and sentenced to 20 years in prison. Instead, Duncan spent a couple of years in a psychiatric program. He's been in and out of prison ever since.

Duncan is now charged with the murder of Dylan, his mother and her boyfriend and another son.

Pedophile-Free Zones Are Needed

Duncan's case is prompting a series of legislative proposals in communities and states across the nation to effectively deal with these killers and molesters.

One of those proposals is to create pedophile-free zones around schools, day care centers, and other places where children are located.

Pedophile-free zones are not the ultimate solution to the problem of child sex offenders, but such efforts send a strong

Traditional Values Coalition Education and Legal Institute, "Special Report: Sympathy For Child Sex Predators," www.traditionalvalues.org, October 2005. Reproduced by permission.

message to sexual predators that the community is watching them and will punish them severely for violating these laws.

Poster Child for Sexual Predators

Steven Elwell is a former high school teacher and a convicted sex offender. Elwell had sexual relations with a 16-year-old girl and spent a year in prison for his crime.

Elwell is now complaining that he and his wife and two children are having a hard time finding a larger house to live in because many communities in New Jersey have passed sex offender-free zones.

Elwell claims he's going to file a civil lawsuit to challenge the constitutionality of one or more of the laws targeting child sex offenders. (Elwell's story was told by an Associated Press reporter and reprinted in papers all over the U.S.)

One of those laws is Megan's Law, which was passed by Congress in 1996 and signed into law by President [Bill] Clinton. Megan's Law requires states to register individuals convicted of sex crimes with the government. A second element requires sex offender information be made available to the public. Many states have set up web sites that list photos, crimes committed, and addresses of paroled or released sex offenders.

Hollywood has . . . promoted sympathy for sex offenders/ child molesters.

Pedophiles Seek Sympathy

A Knight-Ridder reporter has written a sympathetic portrayal about a convicted sex offender named Fred Davis, Jr. Davis was convicted in 1987 for the rape of a pre-teenage girl. According to Davis, he was wrongly convicted and is just "trying to pick up my life and move on." But, according to reporter Rick Armon, "No matter how hard they strive, they say, it remains elusive in a society gripped by fear over high-profile child-kidnapping cases and those who are bent on punishing offenders even after they leave prison."

Armon quotes David A. D'Amora, director of the Center for the Treatment of Problem Sexual Behavior, who thinks that registration legislation may do more harm than good in dealing with sex offenders. He claims that publishing the names and addresses of sex offenders is destabilizing their ability to stay employed and remain in stable housing. "What we think we're doing is creating some protection, but these folks end up in shelters or living on the street where nobody is watching them." . . .

Hollywood has also promoted sympathy for sex offenders/child molesters. Lee Daniels, a homosexual film producer, is the force behind the 2004 film, "The Woodsman," starring Kevin Bacon. The producer told *Film Festival Today* that he wanted to "put a benign face on pedophilia" in this film.

Pedophile-free zones are only one way to hold child molesters accountable for their actions.

Bacon plays a paroled child molester who tries to get his life back on track. Bacon is portrayed sympathetically while his parole officer and therapist are the least likable characters in the film. (Daniels also produced "Shadowboxer," the story of two contract killers—a woman and her stepson—and their sexual relationship.)

In 2004, Hollywood also gave us Nicole Kidman in "Birth." Kidman plays a woman who lost her husband but then comes to believe that a pre-teen boy is her re-incarnated husband. The film shows them bathing together. The film was a box-office flop but is now available in video stores. The pro-pedophilia message is presented in a "reasonable" fashion as a logical outcome of her faulty perceptions.

Sex-Offender-Free Zones

Numerous states or communities have implemented legislation that forbids convicted child sex offenders from living within a thousand feet or more from schools or day care centers. In New Jersey, Elwell plans on challenging the ordinance. Defense attorney John S. Furlong opposes pedophile-free zones. He notes: "These laws have absolutely nothing to do with the protection of children and everything to do with scare tactics, cheap political points and an antiintellectualism that is driving public policy today."

The ACLU [American Civil Liberties Union], of course, opposes pedophile-free zones. It also opposes sex offender registries so citizens can know if a pedophile is living next door to them. The ACLU has also gone on record opposing the use of Global Positioning System technology to track the whereabouts of convicted sex offenders. All of these efforts, say the ACLU, violates the rights of paroled predators.

Pedophile-free zones may be popular vote-getting issues for politicians and may not be totally effective. However, they will provide law enforcement officials with additional legal weapons to use against pedophiles who violate these zones. The public discussion about these zones also serves an educational purpose to keep parents alert to protect their children from sex predators.

Additional Proposals to Protect Children

Pedophile-free zones are only one way to hold child molesters accountable for their actions.

More needs to be done, however. Here are some legislative proposals that should be considered by legislators and community leaders:

- States should abolish statute of limitations on child sex abuse cases.

- States should raise statutory rape laws to at least 16 years of age.

- Professionals should be required by law to turn in sex abusers. This would include doctors, nurses, psychiatrists, teachers, and clergy.

- States should enact a 25-year minimum sentence for first time child sex offenders.

- States and federal government should remove the tax-exempt status of non-profit organizations that hide cases of child abuse inside their organizations. They should take away corporate tax advantages for profit-making organizations that hide child sex abusers. These are a few efforts that can be made to protect our nation's children from sexual predators and killers like Joseph Duncan.

Tougher Sex-Offender Laws May Be Counterproductive

Jason McBride

Jason McBride is a reporter for the Seattle Post-Intelligencer.

Washington [state] lawmakers have joined in the national clamor to get tough on sex offenders with a flurry of proposed legislation that aims to protect children. But victims' advocates fear lawmakers are going too far and could actually hinder prosecutions and leave more sex offenders on the streets.

Fewer Convictions Foreseen

"I worry that when you make penalties more severe, it doesn't lead to more convictions; it leads to fewer," said Lucy Berliner, director of the King County Assault Resource Center.

Lawmakers hope to mirror Jessica's Law, which was passed in Florida [in 2005] after the killing of a 9-year-old girl by an unregistered sex offender living in her neighborhood. The bipartisan effort, led by House Criminal Justice and Corrections [Committee] Chairman Al O'Brien, D-Mountlake Terrace, and Rep. Jay Rodne, R-Snoqualmie, could result in longer sentences, stiffer penalties for sex offenders who don't register with authorities and GPS [global positioning satellite] monitoring for convicted offenders on parole.

Legislators say they were prompted to pass tougher laws after several high-profile cases, particularly the kidnapping of Shasta Groene, 8, and Dylan Groene, 9, in Idaho [in May 2005]. Joseph E. Duncan III, who was arrested when he turned up at a Denny's restaurant with Shasta, is being charged with the kidnapping. Duncan was out on bail on child molestation charges at the time and had a history of similar offenses.

Jason McBride, "Tougher Sex Offender Laws Could Backfire, Advocates Say," *Seattle Post-Intelligencer*, January 9, 2006. Reproduced by permission.

"I think things like that tend to generate attention, and we need to do more," said Rep. John Lovick, D-Mill Creek, who is sponsoring two GPS-monitoring bills.

The centerpiece of the O'Brien-Rodne legislation calls for a 25-years-to-life sentence for violent sex crimes committed against a child younger than 14.

"Under present standards, the guy would probably get 10–12 years in prison," O'Brien said.

Harsher sentencing requirements could discourage victims from testifying.

Victims Would Be Discouraged from Testifying

The concern among [victims'] advocates is that harsher sentencing requirements could discourage victims from testifying, particularly when relatives are the perpetrators. But O'Brien plans to keep intact the Special Sex Offender Sentencing Alternative, which allows prosecutors to go after lighter sentences for offenders who have established relationships with their victims, as long as the crime is not substantially violent and the offender has a clean record.

According to Berliner, most people charged with sexual offenses plead guilty. "When you make penalties so severe, fewer people will plead guilty to that," Berliner said. "You'll end up with some people sent to prison longer, but fewer people sent to prison at all."

Sentencing for sex offenders varies according to the type of crime committed, the offender's criminal history and how likely the offender is to commit another crime. The most serious offenders are civilly committed for rehabilitation after completely serving their sentences. About 200 of these offenders are housed at the Special Commitment Center at McNeil Island Corrections Center near Steilacoom.

Legislation would also extend the statute of limitations on the use of DNA evidence, require out-of-state offenders to register within three days of moving to Washington and force those convicted of possessing child pornography to register as sex offenders.

"We need to do a better job of protecting the public, and we're not, and I think that's what's prompting this legislation," Lovick said.

More Funding Is Needed for Victims

But Mary Ellen Stone, executive director of the King County Sexual Assault Resource Center, said much of the proposed legislation misses the bigger issues, such as the fact that many sexual crimes go unreported.

"[Convicted offenders] represent a small fraction of the sex offenders that are out there," Stone said. "There's got to be both pieces that encourage victims to come forward and get help."

Stone says that funding for victim services are in jeopardy. Hospitals are losing money for forensic rape exams for victims who come to emergency rooms. Stone also said court protection orders tailored to sexual assault victims are needed.

Rodne acknowledged the legislation lacks the components desired by victims' advocates but agreed that those issues need to be covered in the future.

Lie Detector Tests for Pedophiles Are Not Reliable

David Lykken

David Lykken is a behavioral geneticist and professor emeritus at the University of Minnesota.

How do you tell if someone is lying? Easy, according to many of those who should know the answer, such as U.S. government law enforcement and intelligence agencies: hook them up to a polygraph lie detector.

The FBI regularly uses the polygraph in national security investigations, and evidence from it is even admissible in some civilian courts in the U.S. . . .

Polygraphs Are a Type of Voodooism

The trouble is, the polygraph doesn't work—at least, not in any scientific sense. There is plenty of evidence for its inefficacy. A 2002 report by the U.S. National Academy of Sciences even equated polygraph screening with voodooism. Worse, it can lead to serious miscarriages of justice. I have personally been involved in three cases in which men were convicted of murder largely on the basis of polygraph tests and later found to be innocent.

What is it about this decades-old technology that makes it so irresistible? The polygraph "works" by monitoring a person's breathing, blood pressure and electrodermal responses (the extent to which sweat changes the electrical conductivity of the skin in the palm of the hand) while an interrogator questions them. All this determines is that the person was relatively more aroused by one question than another. It cannot determine why a question aroused them, or whether this was

David Lykken, "Nothing like the Truth," *New Scientist*, vol. 183, August 14, 2004, p 17.

due to guilt, fear or irritation. Indeed, biting your tongue or clenching your toes can elicit similar physiological responses and create polygraph readings that are indistinguishable from involuntary ones.

[Polygraph] research is inadequate on several counts.

To determine whether a person's response to an accusing question signifies deception, the examiner must set a baseline level by asking them leading questions designed to induce a relatively low arousal response. Since the 1950s, the standard format for this has been the Control Question Test (CQT), in which questions relevant to the investigation (such as "During May this year, did you take 4-year-old Tommy's penis in your mouth?" —an actual question from one of the cases in which I testified) are intermixed with control questions about minor misdeeds the person may have committed in the past (such as "Have you ever told a lie to get out of trouble?").

The theory is that an innocent person, able to answer the relevant questions truthfully, will be more disturbed by the control questions and show stronger physiological reactions to them, whereas a guilty person will react most strongly to the relevant questions.

Polygraph Research Is Inadequate

A newer version of the CQT is the Directed Lie Test, in which the baseline is set by asking the subject to deny common sins such as whether they have ever exceeded the speed limit. Again, this assumes that people who answer the relevant questions truthfully will be more disturbed by having to lie about minor misdeeds.

Polygraph examiners claim accuracy rates of between 95 and 99 per cent. However, these claims are not supported by credible research. True, guilty suspects who fail polygraph tests sometimes feel compelled to confess, and these confessions can confirm the innocence of other suspects who passed their polygraph tests. Another examiner can then blindly rescore the tests to determine their accuracy. Research on the validity of polygraph tests is based almost entirely on these cases.

But this research is inadequate on several counts. Most guilty suspects who fail the test do not confess, and studies based on confessions always overestimate the validity of the polygraph because they exclude results both from guilty suspects who passed the test and from innocent suspects who would have failed had investigators carried on testing alternative suspects after finding one who lied—something they rarely do.

Four such studies of polygraph accuracy have been published in scientific journals since 1976, and the results are not encouraging. Innocent suspects were recorded as "deceptive" in 47 per cent of cases. You'd barely get a better result with the flip of a coin. Clearly, polygraph tests are strongly biased against the truthful person. Guilty suspects, on the other hand, can easily learn to fool the polygraph by artificially raising their physiological responses to the control questions, say by pressing their foot on a tack they have secreted in their shoe. They will then appear to be more disturbed by the control questions than by the relevant questions. Despite the fact that a lie detector in Washington D.C. is about as useless as a compass at the magnetic North Pole, the U.S. government continues to be the most enthusiastic user. It has even started using computers to measure and score the responses from polygraph tests. Marrying the myth of the lie detector with the mystique of the computer has spawned a progeny of mythlets that have compromised U.S. intelligence findings and victimised honourable people.

Women Should Not Be Prosecuted for Fetal Abuse

Austin Reed Cline

Austin Reed Cline is a regional director for the Council for Secular Humanism and a former publicity coordinator for the Campus Freethought Alliance.

Should women who abuse drugs while they are pregnant be charged with delivery of drugs to a minor and child abuse after their baby is born? There is an increasing movement among prosecutors and conservative politicians to do exactly that, leading to growing numbers of women who are charged and convicted of child abuse which occurred before their child was even a part of society.

The Legal Status of a Fetus Has Been Elevated

South Carolina seems to be at the forefront of this movement, but other states like Arizona are following suit. As far back as 1996, the South Carolina Supreme Court upheld the conviction of a woman who had used crack cocaine during the third trimester of her pregnancy. The defendant in *South Carolina v. Whitner* had argued that her fetus did not meet the definition of "child" under the law, but the Court found that because the fetus was viable, it qualified.

In another case (*Ferguson v. Charleston, South Carolina*), a public hospital in South Carolina had been testing women for drug use without their knowledge and turning the women over to the police if the blood work came back positive. Many were convicted of child abuse, but in 2001, the U.S. Supreme Court ruled against the state and the hospital.

Austin Reed Cline, "Drug Use & Fetal Abuse: What Legal Status Should a Fetus Have?" http://atheism.about.com. Reproduced by permission.

These cases reflect an interesting intersection between the conservative War on Drugs and the conservative effort to restrict reproductive freedoms. With the former, punishment is preferred over treatment while with the latter, a fetus is thought to merit the same moral and legal status as a newborn.

Why should the government stop with the abuse of drugs? Why not treat any actions of a pregnant woman exactly as if they were done by a mother?

Who Should Be Prosecuted?

The images of drug-addicted babies with profound birth defects, assuming that they are born alive at all, may readily incline us to agree with such prosecutions of women who abuse drugs during pregnancy. There is no question that these infants are suffering for no good reason and that their mothers have done something horribly wrong in exposing their fetuses to harmful drugs. But does this mean that prosecution for child abuse is warranted?

We should set aside for a moment the most extreme cases and consider the implications for more likely situations. For example, in the case of *Crawley v. Catoe* a woman was charged and convicted of child endangerment because of drug use during pregnancy, even though she gave birth to a perfectly healthy baby. Should she really be punished, even though her baby experienced no harm?

If such prosecutions are based upon valid principles, why should the government stop with the abuse of drugs? Why not treat any actions of a pregnant woman exactly as if they were done by a mother? For example, a woman who drinks alcohol or smokes at any time during pregnancy could be prosecuted just as if she had given alcohol or cigarettes to a child. Why not? After all, the harm experienced by fetuses from drugs like cocaine have been found to be speculative, overstated, and in general simply pale in comparison to the harms from nicotine and alcohol.

Because such actions often do not result in any obvious or even actual harm, if the government wishes to prevent them it will have to engage in more active monitoring of pregnant women. Perhaps hospitals should be required to perform blood tests on all pregnant women and give the results to the authorities. Of course, even women who do not yet know that they are pregnant can still harm their fetuses, so perhaps the government should monitor all women of child-bearing age.

Then again, perhaps it would be more cost efficient to simply force all women to use a contraceptive like Norplant and thus only test those who have been given permission to be fertile. If this sounds paranoid, it's not; a number of judges across the country have given women who have abused drugs during pregnancy a choice between Norplant and jail, all in the name of protecting the interests of their theoretical and un-conceived children.

There are a number of moral problems with prosecuting any women who abuse drugs during pregnancy.

Fear of Prosecution Discourages Prenatal Care

One obvious result of such draconian measures would be that more and more women will stay away from healthcare providers, especially if they know they are pregnant, out of fear of what could happen. This is already a consequence for women who abuse drugs—and they are the last people who should be going without proper prenatal care! This could also encourage women to have unsafe, late-term abortions rather than risk the pregnancy coming to term, an ironic situation considering that those who support these prosecutions also generally oppose legal abortion as well.

As we can see, there are a number of moral problems with prosecuting any women who abuse drugs during pregnancy. From a utilitarian perspective, it results in a number of consequences which can have the opposite effect intended—when women avoid doctors out of fear of jail, both they and their babies will be in greater danger from a wide range of medical problems. There is also a serious problem with the prospect of women losing the ability to trust their healthcare providers as doctors are forced to move from treatment to punishment as a solution to addiction.

Women who use drugs during pregnancy do not do so out of an active desire to harm their fetus.

Drug addiction is a complicated social issue. Women who use drugs during pregnancy do not do so out of an active desire to harm their fetus. Punishment through prosecution and jail, especially with the aid of doctors and nurses, seems an unlikely means to effectively combat either problem, and it certainly doesn't appear to have a sound moral basis.

Organizations to Contact

ACT for Kids
7 S. Howard St., Suite 200, Spokane, WA 99201-3816
(866) 348-5437 • fax: (509) 747-0609
e-mail: resources@actforkids.org
Web site: www.actforkids.org

ACT for Kids is a nonprofit organization that provides resources, consultation, research, and training for the prevention and treatment of child abuse and sexual violence. The organization publishes workbooks, manuals, and books such as *He Told Me Not to Tell* and *How to Survive the Sexual Abuse of Your Child*.

**American Academy of Child and
Adolescent Psychiatry (AACAP)**
3615 Wisconsin Ave. NW, Washington, DC 20016-3007
(202) 966-7300 • fax: (202) 966-2891
Web site: www.aacap.org

AACAP is a nonprofit organization that supports and advances child and adolescent psychiatry through research and the distribution of information. The academy's goal is to provide information that will remove the stigma associated with mental illnesses and assure proper treatment for children who suffer from mental or behavioral disorders due to child abuse or other factors. AACAP publishes fact sheets on a variety of issues concerning disorders that may affect children and adolescents. Titles include "Child Sexual Abuse" and "Child Abuse—the Hidden Bruises."

American Bar Association (ABA)

Center on Children and the Law, Washington, DC 20005
(202) 622-1720 • fax: (202) 662-1755
e-mail: ctrchildlaw@abanet.org
Web site: www.abanet.org

The ABA Center on Children and the Law aims to improve the quality of life for children through advances in law and public policy. It publishes the monthly *ABA Child Law Practice* and specialized information on legal matters related to the protection of children, including the book *Keeping Kids Out of the System*.

Americans for Religious Liberty (ARL)

P.O. Box 6656, Silver Spring, MD 20916
(301) 260-2988 • fax: (301) 260-2989
e-mail: arlinc@erols.com
Web site: www.arlinc.org

ARL, founded in 1982, is dedicated to defending religious liberty, church-state separation, and reproductive rights through research, litigation, education, and publications, including ARL's quarterly journal, *Voice of Reason*.

Association for the Rights of Catholics in the Church (ARCC)

PO Box 85, Southampton, MA 01073
(413) 527-9929 • fax: (413) 527-5877
e-mail: arccangel@charter.net
Web site: www.arcc-catholic-rights.org

Founded in 1980 by lay and clerical Catholics, ARCC's primary goal is to promote accountability, institutionalize shared decision making, and preserve the rights of all Catholics. On its Web site ARCC provides access to archives of its newsletter *ARCC Light* and documents written by ARCC members, including "Vatican Must Deal Openly with Priest Pedophilia Cases."

Association of Sites Advocating Child Protection (ASACP)

5042 Wilshire Blvd., #540, Los Angeles, CA   90036-4305

(323) 908-7864

email: comments@asacp.org

Web site: www.asacp.org

ASACP is a nonprofit organization dedicated to eliminating child pornography from the Internet. ASACP battles child pornography through its reporting hotline and by organizing the efforts of the online adult industry to combat child sexual abuse.

Center for Effective Discipline (CED)

155 W. Main St., Suite 1603, Columbus, OH   43215

(614) 221-8829 • fax: (614) 221-2110

e-mail: info@StopHitting.org

Web site: www.stophitting.org

The CED provides educational information to the public on the effects of corporal punishment of children and alternatives to its use. It is also the headquarters for End Physical Punishment of Children, or EPOCH-USA. The center publishes guidelines for parents, which are available from its Web site, including "10 Guidelines for Raising a Well-Behaved Child."

Child Welfare League of America (CWLA)

440 First St. NW, 3rd Foor,, Washington, DC   20001-2085

(202) 638-2952 • fax: (202) 638-4004

Web site: www.cwla.org

The Child Welfare League of America is an association of more than seven hundred public and private agencies and organizations devoted to improving the lives of children. CWLA publications include the book *Tender Mercies: Inside the World of a Child Abuse Investigator*, the quarterly magazine *Children's Voice*, and the bimonthly journal *Child Welfare*.

False Memory Syndrome Foundation

1955 Locust St., Philadelphia, PA   19103-5766
(215) 940-1040 • fax: (215) 940-1042
e-mail: mail@fmsfonline.org
Web site: www.fmsfonline.org

The foundation believes that many "delayed memories" of sexual abuse are the result of false memory syndrome (FMS). In FMS, patients in therapy "recall" childhood abuse that never occurred. The foundation seeks to discover reasons for the spread of FMS, works for the prevention of new cases, and aids FMS victims, including those falsely accused of abuse. The foundation publishes a newsletter and various papers and distributes articles and information on FMS.

Family Violence and Sexual Assault Institute (FVSAI)

6160 Cornerstone Ct. East, San Diego, CA   92121
(858) 623-2777 ext. 406 • fax: (858) 646-0761
e-mail: fvsai@alliant.edu
Web site: www.fvsai.org

The FVSAI networks among people and agencies involved in studying, treating, protecting, or otherwise dealing with violent or abusive families. On its Web site the FVSAI sponsors a book club that includes FVSAI's bibliographies, treatment manuals, and other books. Publications include the bibliographies *Sexual Abuse/Incest Survivors* and *Child Physical Abuse/Neglect* and the quarterly *Family Violence and Sexual Assault Bulletin*.

Klaas Kids Foundation

PO Box 925, Sausalito, CA   94966
(415) 331-6867 • fax: (415) 331-5633
e-mail: klaaskids@pacbell.net
Web site: www.klaaskids.org

The Klaas Kids Foundation was established in 1994 after the death of twelve-year-old kidnapping and murder victim Polly Klaas. The foundation's goal is to acknowledge that crimes against children deserve a high priority and to form partnerships with concerned citizens, the private sector, organizations, law enforcement, and legislators to fight crimes against children. The foundation publishes the quarterly newsletter *Klaas Action Review.*

Male Survivor
5505 Connecticut Ave. NW, Washington, DC   20015-2601
(800) 738-4181
Web site: www.malesurvivor.org

Male Survivor, formerly the National Organization on Male Sexual Victimization, believes that sexually victimized boys and men need added support to come forward and ask for help. Identification, assessment, and intervention help prevent abused boys from becoming self-destructive or abusive adolescents and men. The organization, which respects the diversity of sexual abuse survivors, serves anyone who has been sexually abused. Male Survivor helps the public and the media to recognize and understand males who have been sexually abused and promotes action to confront and fight male sexual abuse. The Male Survivor Web site provides information for survivors, clinicians, and caregivers. It also provides access to news and publishes *Male Survivor,* its quarterly newsletter.

National Center for Missing and Exploited Children (NCMEC)
699 Prince St., Alexandria, VA   22314
(800) THE LOST
Web site: www.missingkids.com

The NCMEC serves as a clearinghouse of information on missing and exploited children and coordinates child protection efforts with the private sector. A number of publications on these issues are available, including guidelines for parents whose children are testifying in court, help for abused children, and booklets such as *Child Molesters: A Behavioral Analysis* and *Child Pornography: It's a Crime.*

National Center for Prosecution of Child Abuse
American Prosecutors Research Institute
   Alexandria, VA   22314
(703) 549-9222 • fax: (703) 836-3195
e-mail: ncpca@ndaa-apri.org
Web site: www.ndaa-apri.org/apri/programs/ncpca/ncpca_
home.html

The center seeks to improve the investigation and prosecution of child abuse cases. As a clearinghouse on child abuse laws and court reforms, the center supports research on reducing courtroom trauma for child victims. It publishes the monthly newsletter *Update*, as well as monographs, bibliographies, special reports, and *Investigation and Prosecution of Child Abuse*, a manual for prosecutors.

National Clearinghouse on Child Abuse and
Neglect Information (NCCANCH)
1250 Maryland Ave. SW, 8th Floor,, Washington, DC   20024
(800) 394-3366 • fax: (703) 385-3206
e-mail: nccanch@caliber.com
Web site: http://nccanch.acf.hhs.gov

This national clearinghouse, an office of the U.S. Department of Health and Human Services, collects, catalogs, and disseminates information on all aspects of child maltreatment, including identification, prevention, treatment, public awareness, training, and education. NCCANCH offers various reports, fact sheets, and bulletins concerning child abuse and neglect.

National Criminal Justice Reference Service (NCJRS)
PO Box 6000, Rockville, MD   20849-6000
(800) 851-3420 • fax: (301) 519-5212
e-mail: askncjrs@ncjrs.org
Web site: www.ncjrs.org

NCJRS is a research and development agency of the U.S. Department of Justice established to prevent and reduce crime and to improve the criminal justice system. Among its publications are *Permanency Planning for Abused and Neglected Children* and *When Your Child Is Missing: A Family Survival Guide.*

Survivor Connections

52 Lyndon Rd., Cranston, RI 02905-1121
(401) 941-2548 • fax: (401) 941-2335
email: survivorconnections@cox.net
Web site: http://members.cox.net/survivorconnections/

Survivor Connections is an activist center for survivors of incest, rape, sexual assault, and child molestation. It publishes the *Survivor Activist,* a newsletter available through regular mail.

United Fathers of America (UFA)

1511 Third Ave., Suite 903, Melbourne Tower
Seattle, WA 98101
(206) 623-5050 • fax: (206) 623-3933
email: mack@isomedia.com
Web site: www.ufa.org

UFA helps fathers fight for the right to remain actively involved in their children's upbringing after divorce or separation. UFA believes that children should not be subject to the emotional and psychological trauma caused when vindictive parents falsely charge ex-spouses with sexually abusing their children. Primarily a support group, UFA answers specific questions and suggests articles and studies that illustrate its position.

VOICES in Action

8041 Hosbrook Rd., Suite 236, Cincinnati, OH 45236
(800) 786-4238
e-mail: voicesinaction@aol.com
Web site: www.voices-action.org

Victims of Incest Can Emerge Survivors (VOICES) provides assistance to victims of incest and child sexual abuse and promotes awareness about the prevalence of incest. It publishes a bibliography and the newsletter *Chorus.*

Bibliography

Books

Cynthia Crosson-Tower

Understanding Child Abuse and Neglect. Boston: Allyn & Bacon, 2004.

Karen A. Duncan

Healing from the Trauma of Childhood Sexual Abuse: The Journey for Women. Westport, CT: Praeger, 2004.

Lois Einhorn

Forgiveness and Child Abuse: Would You Forgive? Bandon, OR: Robert D. Reed, 2006.

Katrina Kittle

The Kindness of Strangers. New York: Morrow, 2006.

Carolyn Lehman

Strong at the Heart: How It Feels to Heal from Sexual Abuse. New York: Farrar, Straus and Giroux, 2005.

Martin Moran

The Tricky Part: A Boy's Story of Sexual Trespass, a Man's Journey to Forgiveness. Boston: Beacon, 2005.

Richard Pelzer

A Brother's Journey: Surviving a Childhood of Abuse. New York: Warner, 2005.

Madelaine Pinkus-Rohn

Charred Souls: A Story of Recreational Child Abuse. Indianapolis: Oberpark, 2002.

Dorothy Rabinowitz	*No Crueler Tyrannies: Accusation, False Witness, and Other Terrors of Our Times.* New York: Free Press, 2003.
Laura Schlessinger	*Bad Childhood, Good Life.* New York: HarperCollins, 2006.
Wayne Theodore	*Wayne: An Abused Child's Story of Courage, Survival, and Hope.* Gig Harbor, WA: Harbor, 2003.
Andrew Turnell and Suzanne Essex	*Working with Denied Child Abuse: The Resolutions Approach.* Berkshire, UK: Open University Press, 2006.
Carla Van Dam	*Socially Skilled Child Molester: Differentiating the Guilty from the Falsely Accused.* Binghamton, NY: Haworth Maltreatment and Trauma Press, 2006.
Marilyn Van Derbur	*Miss America by Day: Lessons Learned from Ultimate Betrayals and Unconditional Love.* Denver: Oak Hill Ridge, 2003.
Walker Young	*A Bruised Child: A Story of Emotional Child Abuse and the Courage to Heal.* Mustang, OK: Tate, 2006.

Periodicals

Paula Andruss	"A Sex Offender Lives on Our Block," *Parents*, July 2004.
David Bahr	"Mothered," *Gentlemen's Quarterly*, August 2004.

Robert Barker "Psychiatric Solutions: You Might Be Shocked," *Business Week*, August 2, 2004.

Biotech Week "McMaster University: More Effort Needed to Prevent Pattern of Child Abuse Developing in Families," May 25, 2005.

Jessica Blatt "I Was Molested by My Cousin," *Cosmo Girl*, November 2005.

Irene Daria-Wiener "Sex Abuse in the Suburbs," *Parents*, July 2004.

Amy Engeler "Is Your Child a Target? The Sex Offender Next Door," *Good Housekeeping*, May 2005.

Kathleen Guton "Safe-Keeping," *America*, February 13, 2006.

Bill Hewitt and Maria Eftimiades "Safe Haven or House of Horror?" *People*, February 13, 2006.

Bill Hewitt, Barbara Sandler, and David Searls "Why Did These Kids Live in Cages?" *People*, October 3, 2005.

Archie Kalokerinos "Abuse or Infection?" *New Scientist*, September 10, 2005.

Katy Kelly "To Protect the Innocent," *U. S. News & World Report*, June 13, 2005.

Will Knight "Chasing the Elusive Shadows of e-Crime," *New Scientist*, May 8, 2004.

Hara Marano — "My Boyfriend Is Mean to My Kids," *Psychology Today*, January/February 2005.

James G. McManus — "Plenty of Blame to Go Around in Crisis: Legal Expert Looks at the Status of Lawsuits and the Church," *National Catholic Reporter*, February 7, 2003.

Susannah Meadows et al. — "Arrested Development," *Newsweek*, November 10, 2003.

Obesity, Fitness & Wellness Week — "Domestic Violence; Pediatricians' Opinions Vary on Reporting Threshold for Suspected Child Abuse," July 30, 2005.

Judith Reisman — "From Greatest Generation to Porn Generation," *Human Events*, June 27, 2005.

Lynn Rosellini — "Get Out of That Car!" *Reader's Digest*, December 2005.

Jessica S. Sachs — "Preventing the Unthinkable," *Parenting*, October 2003.

Catharine Skipp and Dirk Johnson — "Brianna: The Little Girl That Could," *Newseek*, October 13, 2003.

Robin D. Stone et al. — "Sexual Abuse," *Jet*, April 5, 2004.

Margaret Talbot — "The Bad Mother," *New Yorker*, August 9, 2004.

Alan X and Amy Hammel-Zabin — "The Mind of a Child Molester," *Psychology Today*, August 2003.

Nir Yativ   "Nanny, Lies, and Videotape: Child Abuse and Privacy Rights Dilemmas," *Pediatrics*, July 1, 2005.

Index